April 28, 1984

Dear Claire,

Happy Polasca. Thank
you for the part you have
played in the development
of my spirituality.

Love,

Michaele

Holistic Spirituality

Holistic Spirituality

John Carmody

PAULIST PRESS
New York/Ramsey

Library of Congress Catalog Card Number: 83-62468

ISBN: 0-8091-2564-1

Published by Paulist Press
545 Island Road, Ramsey, N.J. 07446

Printed and bound in the United States of America

Contents

for the Wichita Liturgy Group:

*Denise Carmody, Gena De Aragon,
Peggy Hartman, Richard Hartman, Kay Maher,
Tom Maher, Carol Richardson,
Jim Snyder, Nancy Snyder*

Preface

This book sketches a Christian spirituality in holistic terms, emphasizing the centrality of God's love and the interconnectedness of the different dimensions of the ordinary believer's life. It touches all the major domains of human existence (nature, society, the self, and God), taking such concerns as ecology, economics, health, and prayer as candidates for Jesus' twofold commandment of love. I'd like to thank Larry Boadt, C.S.P., of Paulist Press for suggesting the book; Kay Maher of Wichita State University's College of Health Related Professions and Hugh Riordan, Director of the Olive W. Garvey Center for the Improvement of Human Functioning, for medical perspectives; Denise Lardner Carmody, for help with feminist issues and support on the home front; and Karla Kraft, for expert typing. In dedicating the book to my own grass-roots Christian community, I mean gratefully to spotlight the local place where Christian faith has become most whole for me.

1

Chapter One
Theological Horizons

What Is a Holistic Spirituality?

A holistic spirituality is a religious outlook and regimen that emphasizes the connections among a person's various interests, problems, and responsibilities. As religious, it stresses the ultimate questions that make all human beings potential philosophers, beginning lovers of wisdom: How do things hang together? Where am I going? What is most important in my life? Taking note of these questions, of their inalienable call to make sense of their time, people develop an outlook in which they are "bound" *(religata)* to the Mystery of life, the primordial reality Western civilization has named "God." If they are serious about answering this call and sense that such binding might be the liberation of their deepest self, they will do something systematic, disciplined, regular about clarifying their ultimate questions. They will put together a regime, a schedule that provides for the key factors they must deal with. Let us agree to call such a regime a "spirituality."

When a spirituality emphasizes the connections among the different concerns that a person must consider, it knocks on the door of holism. Holism (or wholism) is an aspiration to deal with one's life adequately, giving each significant factor its due. Work and love, prayer and politics, sex and social service—each of the many ingredients or dimensions in our average American lives clamors for attention. If we are not to become swamped, we have to make our peace with this clamor, hush it to a manageable level of decibels. That requires hard choices about what is central and what is peripheral—hard choices that will never be far from our reflections here. On the other hand, if the surgery we perform to keep our nerves from overloading is not to leave us crippled, we must take pains to keep our central concerns sufficiently connected, both to one another and to our many peripheral concerns, to maintain a balance or roundness. In a word, we must honor the need we all feel to be whole.

So, this book is concerned with wholeness, and its first thesis is that wholeness begins with religion. As Aristotle taught generations of traditional Westerners, the end is the first in the order of causes. Since religion deals with the end of things, that Mystery which death makes it imperative for all of us to consider, religion is the wise person's abiding interest. Psychologist Erik Erikson has spoken of wisdom as the elderly person's peculiar virtue, the strength required of those who have approached the end of their time and must muster the capacity to love life in the face of death. But all of us have bones set for wisdom; we all need to wonder about where we are going. All of us hunger for the order, the sense of plan, that a view "under the aspect of eternity" might provide. Psychiatrist Robert Coles has shown this in the case of a little girl growing up in a rich household of New Orleans. As the black maid who was the little girl's closest friend described the girl's condition:

> She wonders about life, and what it's about, and what the end of things will be. That's good. But she's stopping now, that's what they [the girl's parents] want: no looking, no staring, no peeking at life. No questions; they don't want questions. They go to church a couple of times a year, Christmas and Easter, and no one asks them any questions there. No one asks them questions anyplace they go.[1]

A large part of our task in this book will be to keep asking questions. I hope that our questions will not be nagging or useless, irritants rather than aids. I hope that the issues we probe will be alive in most readers' consciousness. And, above all, I hope that our questions will conduce to peeking at life, wondering what the end of things will be. If they do, they will take us to the border of prayer, where we lift our minds and hearts up to God, the holy Mystery, giving thanks for the light of our eyes and the air we breathe, begging our daily bread and the forgiveness of our sins, finally growing quiet, whole, reknit by leaving even holy busyness aside and simply loving God, communing with God, heart to heart.

In loving God heart to heart, the traditional Christian of simpler ages found a center, a still point of the turning world. The love of God, with whole mind, heart, soul, and strength, was Jesus' first command, and like to it was Jesus' second command, the love of neighbor as oneself. Conjoined, these loves were like the hub of a wheel, a center from which all other duties or preoccupations could radiate like spokes. Because they had a common reference point, the same central source, the spokes could be ordered and cooperative. If each bore its load, the person's time would turn steadily, carrying him forward, making for genuine progress. So one talked of Christian faith as "the way," or one read Bonaventure on the itinerary of the mind's ascent to God, or Bunyan's *Pilgrim's Progress* graced the center of one's bookcase. Traditionally, wholeness and progress were thought equally possible, joint ingredients in religious living.

The task for us, in a more complicated time, is to keep the flames of such hope leaping. How can we, with all the assaults on our consciousness, all the importunings of our time and money, find a path, an outlook, a regime that will integrate our lives sufficiently to give us a sense of a growing wholeness, an increasing peace? That is the tall question a holistic spirituality sets out to answer.

The Life-Cycle

Providentially, a holistic spirituality has time on its side. As a mercy of God, something in our inner clocks pressures us to answer the tall question of integrity or wholeness. From the

beginnings of our physical and mental growth, as Jean Piaget
and other psychologists have discovered, we are concerned with
adding to our repertoire of skills, consolidating our muscular
and mental achievements. Our growth, therefore, is not so much
linear as spiral. We do not progress in a straight line; we go back
over the same materials, again and again, gradually lifting them
up into higher syntheses. In intellectual terms, this is the phenomenon of achieving a series of higher viewpoints. Thus 1776
continues to connote the American Revolution, but the significance of the American Revolution changes dramatically as we
pass from a child's studies in junior high to a history major's
studies in college, from a history major's studies in college to the
lectures of a young professor, from the lectures of a young professor to the masterwork of an emeritus scholar capping a life's
worth of meditation. While 1776 is still 1776, it means so much
more to the emeritus scholar than to the junior high student that
it scarcely seems the same year.

So too with ourselves. In the history of Mary Doe, alter ego
or forthright self, a similar procession of higher viewpoints can
occur. This may not be readily apparent if we look for it every
day, but if we ask who Mary Doe is at twenty, and then at forty,
and then at sixty, and then at eighty, we likely will receive significantly different answers. Throughout she will remain the
dutiful daughter of Donald and Dora, but at twenty she'll be
auburn-haired and intense, at forty she'll be knowing and motherly, at sixty she'll be attuned to the seasons, at eighty she'll be
prowling with the grey panthers. "If I had known then what I
know now," she'll follow all her forbears in saying. "Oh to be
able to put an old head on young shoulders."

In young adulthood, we search for enough sense of who we
are to let us take our place in the worlds of work and social intercourse. To find this sense of identity, often we have to rebel
against the definitions that our parents or brothers and sisters
imposed. The inadequacies in their worldviews and selves being
quite apparent, we decide that ours will be a quite different way.
Later, when the inadequacies in our own ways have also become
apparent, we may look back on our parents or siblings more
kindly. But at the time when all the voices, both the demons

within and the furies without, insist that we proclaim who we are, we are almost sure to make part of our answer: "I am not the blocks that chipped me."

Beyond individual identity, however, lies intimacy, the bonding of two somewhat achieved personalities. Intimacy both requires a sense of self and enhances that sense. Through the loves of friendship and romance, we give and take the revelations that make our selves interesting. Usually this process takes us into marriage, the commitment to make a love that is ongoing, a life that fully shares whatever may come. So the partners to a marriage take one another for better or worse, richer or poorer, in sickness and health, until death do them part. Instinctively, they suspect that their sharings of bed and board are both the most delicate and the most fruitful kind of knowing. Thus Adam knew Eve and a fateful progeny got going. Thus any of us who reflects will marvel at the wealth of implication a mere shrug can carry across the dinner table.

Once people are bonded, married, set forth on their adventure in sharing, they usually become concerned about the fruitfulness of their life time. Through love, they usually raise up children, somehow managing to bear the big worries and responsibilities of such little ones. Through work, they usually contribute to the common welfare, making things that others need, staffing institutions that keep things going. This is all quite commonplace, just ordinary parenting and ordinary laboring, yet it is all quite profound. For through it occur such macro-wonders as economics, evolution, and social history. Year after year, men sleep with women, workers collaborate, teachers toil with students, nurses bind up wounds, mothers dandle babies—and thereby *homo sapiens* takes another step on the strange pilgrimage God started. Seeing that start, the morning stars sang together and all the angels of God shouted for joy (Job 38:7). In the tracks of that start, even such a mediocre middle-ager as Rabbit Angstrom, novelist John Updike's very modest alter ego, takes on an aura of potent significance.[2] If Rabbit says sooth, any of us may come to middle age with stories eye has never before seen, ear has never before heard, the heart has never before conceived.

Yet, knowing his own New Testament, God seems to have saved the best wine till last. After fifty, Aristotle found, one has enough experience to know something about *phronesis*, prudence or instinctive ethics. By that time, the psychologist C.G. Jung discovered, people's crises become religious: they must make sense of an hourglass running out. So, many older people become reflective, regularly thinking on the end of things. A day is no longer simply for doing, achieving. A day is now for appreciating, savoring. Cleared of some of its earlier clutter, the older consciousness can grow sacramental, setting such trifles as a cool breeze or a brisk tea in the frame of the Creator's comprehensive giving. At that point, things are coming together, summing up, making a whole. Maybe a holistic spirituality is nothing more than Plato's old definition of philosophy: the art of dying.

Jesus

For the Christian, the art of dying, and the art of living, took classical form in Jesus of Nazareth. Even since Jesus' passover from suffering the effects of sin to enjoying the effulgence of divine grace, Christians' life-stories have been measured by Jesus' frame. What is Christians' deepest identity? They are children of God, brothers and sisters of the Christ, members of a body in which there is neither Jew nor Gentile, slave nor free, male nor female. This is the identity promised them at baptism, confirmed when they come of age, nourished at each sharing in the Lord's Supper. Though it may take them to their last breath to grasp even a portion of this identity, Jesus lays it before them bountifully. "You shall not die but live," the Word of God assures them. "This place is for you no lasting city."

What is the Christian's best intimacy? Once again, Jesus stimulates the answers. As Jesus walked with his God, learning through time what the Abba wanted, so the Christian may walk with God, trusting that the divine parenthood will prove trustworthy. The intimacy of Jesus with his Father, so great that he and the Father were one, gives Christians their model of religious perfection, and their model of marriage as well. If the person who saw Jesus saw the Father, as the Johannine writings proclaim, so, in paler fashion, the person who sees a true Christian glimpses the Father of lights. And as Jesus laid down his life for his friends, to cap a career of public service, so a Christian husband lays down his life for his wife, a Christian friend spends himself for his friends. This need not be dramatic or crucifying. It need only be real: a growing tendency day by day to consider the other's welfare even more important than one's own.

How does the mature, generative Christian appear? Very much in the lineaments of Jesus. The love and work that Freud made the key indices of mental health blaze forth in Jesus' charismatic appeal to society's marginal people, Jesus' bone-wearying labor to lay the foundations of a new era in which God might powerfully reign. Greater love than that, the Christian Scriptures were sure, never had appeared. More creative and effective work never would follow. Jesus was so profound in his love that a new order of being came forth. Thenceforth, nothing could separate human beings from the love of God, because the love of God, God's own being, would be human beings' inmost reality. Jesus was so creative in his work that it restructured history. To this day, there are more Christians than adherents of any other set of beliefs, and tracks the world over bear the imprint of Jesus' hammering: One thing alone is necessary. In Jesus' followers, this one thing marks all honorable generativity. Entrusting themselves to God, mature Christians love and work freely, joyously, as though God were the major stockholder in all their business. In Ignatius Loyola's formula, mature Christians pray as if everything depended on themselves and work as if everything depended on God. Note the contrast to our modern inclinations.

And, last, what is the Christian wisdom that the last stages of the life-cycle should sponsor? Nothing but the ability to love life in the face of Jesus' cross. Where Jesus disarmed the strong man Satan, taking away his power to eviscerate our human hopes, the wise Christian disarms the cynic and shallow sophisticate, daring to believe that love is stronger than death. The evil that Christ suffered, the agony of Christ's outstretched arms, shows the sobriety in Christian redemption, the repudiation of any cheap grace. It is the law of the cross that God has made statutory for redemption. By Jesus' stripes we were healed. Yet where sin abounded grace has abounded the more, so the Christian's last anointing says *yes*. Yes, there is far more in God's creation to admire than to despise. Yes, my life, despite all my stupidities and sins, stands as a tribute to God's goodness. Even though my heart condemns me, God is greater than my heart, and God knows all. Let me praise him all my days.

In traditional Christian spirituality, the imitation of Christ was crucial. As one slowly put on Christ's mind, these extrinsic or descriptive similarities that we have been sketching gave way to an intrinsic identification. So Paul came to think that he no longer lived in his own right. What was important in his later years was the living of Christ in him. To live was Christ and to die was gain, because Christ was his blood and marrow. The analogy for most of us is hard to summon, so far are we from Paul's passion, but it at least beckons to us from the evangelists' portraits of Jesus, taking the form of an invitation. If we wish, if we say yes, there can be a fusion of our lives with Jesus. Personalizing the love of God, Jesus can be for us not just a model but an icon, the Image we bear in our heart of the fathomless love of creation. Not calling us servants but friends, Jesus would disclose the secrets of his heart, the recesses of the divine Mystery. Hard as it is to believe, the disclosure is all acceptance and love. God is so good that he would make his own life the center of our wheeling and dealing. Breaking forth in Jesus' parables and healings, in the sacraments of Jesus' body and the movements of Jesus' Spirit, this divine life would make us whole.

Salvation

The traditional Christian word for healing or making whole is salvation. *Salus*, the root of this word, means health. Therefore, the central process in any holistic spirituality that is Christian is the saving action of Christ and the Spirit. Living in our midst, they would reknit our fragmented psyches, cover over the holes in our souls. Against the forces of original sin, the distortions of the environment into which any of us is born, Christ and the Spirit infiltrate the powers of a new creation. Of course, any creation is a tribute to God's victory over nothingness. The basic question in all philosophies of depth is why there is something rather than nothing. There is something, the Christian says, because God chose to share the divine sufficiency. As an excess, a surplus of the divine love, God chose to express his pure isness into flowers and fields, waves and watermelons. But the most fascinating creations of God are the outflows of the divine love that make rational creatures images of God, similar to their source through a miniature creativity. To accomplish this, God has to persuade human freedom that its consummation comes not from a spurious independence but from turning around to follow the divine light.

When Jesus came on the Israelite scene, as the evangelists report it, he chose to define his mission in terms of a striking text from Isaiah (61:1-2): "The Spirit of the Lord is upon me, because he has anointed me to preach good news to the poor. He has sent me to proclaim release to the captives and recovering of sight to the blind, to set at liberty those who are oppressed, to proclaim the acceptable year of the Lord." In all dimensions of human life, healing, salvation stood ready to hand. The first market for Jesus' work was the marginals of his time, those cast out from the centers of influence and power. Physically and spiritually, the inbreaking of the Father's powerful love, what Jesus called the kingdom of God, would make such marginal individuals people of account, people healthy and important. Contrary to the instincts of the diseased society that had despised them, the new community that Jesus wanted to establish would reverse the distinctions between high and low, worthy and worthless. Behold, Jesus was making all things new. The time had come, the kingdom was at hand. To gain renewal, healing, people had only to repent of their old foolishness and believe in Jesus' glad tidings.

Through two thousand years, all who have heard of Jesus have waited for the flowering of God's kingdom. It has not come, at least in the ways that most waiters have expected. The Church, supposed to incarnate Jesus' saving vision and power, supposed to be a place of radical justice and love, has continued to perpetuate distinctions between high and low, worthy and worthless. To its great shame, the legion of Jesus' followers has not been able to keep even its own house in order. Against its Master's explicit injunction in John 17, the Church has not prized unity above lesser advantages, has not realized that its disunity blocks the world from believing in God's love. So the Church has split and fought and hated furiously, mocking the God of honesty and love it only exists to serve. In part because of the wretched performance of us Christians, the rest of human history has been a nightmare of wars and brutalities. Such inhumanity of human beings to one another can bring our hopes for justice close to extinction. The light has shone in the darkness, and the darkness seems on the verge of snuffing it out.

Yet, of course, this is not the whole story. As Alexsandr Solzhenitsyn eloquently argued in his Nobel acceptance speech, a single word of truth is more powerful than all the lies the world's evil geniuses have been able to muster.[3] For as long as there is a single word of truth, a single act of love, the lies and hatreds stand stripped of their plausibility. The human soul is like a tuning fork, made to resonate to the harmonies of truth and love. Let truth or love once strike the soul and ever after it knows that lies and hatred are unnatural, disordered cacaphonies pointed to hell. It follows, then, that prophets such as Solzhenitsyn, sages such as the Buddha and Socrates, to say nothing of Jesus the definitive Savior, bless our race all out of proportion to their political power or the size of their constituencies. As long as they remain in the human memory, the light holds the darkness at bay. If they continue to appear in our libraries, we still have a choice about which path we will take.

Behold, then: Because of Jesus and Socrates, the Buddha and Solzhenitsyn, God continues to set before us this day two paths, of death and of life. Therefore, let us choose life, the path of honesty and love (Dt 30:15–20). As most of the great exemplars of honesty and love make plain, the way of life is not easy. Still, where else can we go? If we take ourselves to the masters of propaganda, the moguls of money and pride, we find our souls darkening like storm-clouds, our inner peace trickling away. On the other hand, if we give our souls good food, contemplating the stars or chewing the Scriptures, a telltale joy starts to invade us. Surprised by this joy, we glimpse the awesome possibility that salvation is but a spiritual revolution away.

Love

Augustine once described this revolution as turning from love of self to love of God. Where sin seemed to him the love of self unto the contempt of God, grace was the love of God unto the contempt of self. He did not mean that grace carried with it self-hatred. Jesus' "Love your neighbor as yourself" was too central in the New Testament for Augustine to have promoted self-hatred. Rather, he meant the sort of self-effacement that John the Baptist immortalized: "He must increase, I must decrease." The love that works our conversion from the path of death to the path of life is an outgoing passion for God.

Responding to the divine initiatives that filter through our homes and places of work, our churches and times of prayer, we can be led to an intense longing for God, the beauty that makes our hearts ache. In the grip of such love, our selves withdraw to the sidelines. At the center of our field of consciousness is the Mystery of beginning and beyond, the music of all the spheres. Set in this soaring speech, the Mystery may seem exalted or highfalutin'. Brought to mind by the blush of a girl's cheek, made to hover by a child's giggle, the Mystery shows itself ever ready to catch our breath. Nothing could be without the divine love, so the divine love must be as near as the pulse at our throats.

You can look for this love in your own neighborhood, try to spy out its feints and beckonings. In my part of the world, where academic dryness sprouts like weeds, any touch of intellectual savor seems God-sent. Let students take flame with humanistic ideas and I fancy God has breathed forth their inspiration. Let a faculty member turn personal, utter a paragraph from the heart, and I find myself hushed as before a revelation. So much of our students' energy goes into distraction or studying to make money that enthusiasm for an idea, appreciation for something noble in science or art, wafts in like an unexpected breeze. So much of our faculty's energy goes into arid criticism or feckless politicking that a paragraph from the heart seems a valentine. One has to restrain appreciative reactions like these, lest the shy student enthusiast or the unusual faculty revealer be frightened back to business as usual. But in one's heart the reaction can be cheering. There *is* a Spirit moving the imagination and mind to love the life of learning. There *is* a Helper quietly arguing that dissection alone is pathology. How good to sense the moving of this Spirit, the groaning of this Helper in our spirits' depths. With sighs too deep for words, the Spirit lures us to open our hearts, to love the love that moves the stars.

And so with the movements of grace that ease the way between parents and children, old members of a little grassroots community and new. Parents, fearing for their children's safety, wanting them to grow up unsullied and unassaulted, can come on too strong, as though they could build an impregnable security system through rules. When teenagers react negatively to such rules, refusing to obey or glowering in bad grace, parents stand poised between escalating and backing away. In the little pause before they commit themselves to escalation, parents may hear a small still voice of the Spirit call them back to the heart of the matter. The heart of the matter is the love of the child that prompts their parental anxieties. The love of God, which certainly embraces the child, can help them to ease away, make room for a little compromise.

Among adults, where social interactions are smoother outwardly but not always easy inside, the Spirit sharpens instincts of compassion and gratitude, helping people build from small gesture to small gesture until they make a friendship or community. Thus a person coming into a group with the burdens of a divorce, or the burdens of being a newcomer to the area, or the unsymmetry of being single can feel her heart warm to the welcome of older group members, their willingness to open the circle, make room for new points of view. They have sensed enough of her need to reach out with a bit of compassion, a bit of understanding, and if she responds in sensitive kind, two solid stones will soon lie before them, ready to be cemented.

The Spirit works in all these little engagements, as the Tempter works in all the cavities that twinge and bother us. If the great mercies of God, such as thus far keeping us from nuclear destruction, rightfully demand our main thanks, we yet owe secondary thanks for the inspirations, the strengths to risk or endure, that are crucial to the well-being of any family, any church, any collaborative enterprise. The only word adequate to the life that such inspirations bring, the increase that such endurances enable, is love. Love is the energy of life. Love is the power to persevere, keep resisting evil, lay down self-advantage for the common good. "Love is patient and kind; love is not jealous or boastful, it is not arrogant or rude. Love does not insist on its own way; it is not irritable or resentful; it does not rejoice at wrong but rejoices in the right. Love bears all things, believes all things, hopes all things, endures all things. Love never ends" (1 Cor 13:4–8). God is love. God's love can make us whole.

Chapter Two
Ecology

Process and Interconnection

The love of God that would make us whole is the center of the spirituality we are exploring. Come from Jesus, exemplified in his parables and healings, radiant in his resurrection, the love of God poured forth in our hearts by the Spirit is both healing and elevating: *gratia sanans et grata elevans*. As we saw in our first pages, however, a holistic spirituality is also connective. From the central love of God it would extend ties to all the significant dimensions of our lives, like spokes from the hub of a wheel. The ties we consider in this chapter are natural: connections to the physical world, non-human creation. The word that recently has gathered together most of these ties is *ecology:* the web of connections that criss-cross any of our natural habitats.

In its scientific sense, ecology is the study of the systemic relations obtaining in habitats such as the midland plains or the eastern marshes. Thus the Flint Hills of Kansas and the Everglades of Florida are natural subjects of ecology. On a larger scale, ecologists study the connections of all a region's waters, or all a continent's air-patterns, or even all the globe's acid rain. More popularly, ecology has come to connote a concern for the environment, a movement to protect wilderness areas, beaches, deserts, and mountains from the depradations of developers, the toxic destructions of industrial pollution.

The first point that comes to mind when I think of the religious side of ecology is the object lesson it gives us in correlation. If we had any doubt that we are bonded to one another, members of a single body, a long look at nature would suggest more than a few second thoughts. For through and through nature is relational, connected, a tissue of dependencies that weave back and forth like the cane of summer furniture. There is the food chain: grains nourish insects, insects nourish birds and rodents, birds and rodents nourish big cats, big cats nourish (the fantasies of) big hunters, big hunters plant grains. There is the water cycle: rain falls from heavy clouds, seeps into the earth, descends to deep aquifers, rises in streams and lakes, runs down to the sea, returns to the clouds in evaporation. If we place a power plant too close to the coastal waters, it overheats the spawning ground of delicate species and so changes the local population of fish, the local economy, the politics and culture of whole counties. When an energetic bunch of developers opened a canal to the Great Lakes, and new species of predatory fish (lampreys) gained access to the inland waters, the old species good for eating soon withered away, taking with them the fishing industry of several states. And so with dozens of other examples, from Love Canal to off-shore drilling. In ecology, if not economics, the trickle-down effect is a fact.

Natural reality is not only interconnected, it is also processive, on the move, ever-changing. Partly through environmental changes, and partly through genetic mutations, all plants, animals, and their habitats keep inching forward or drifting to the side. The prodigal numbers that Annie Dillard reported for insect life, the buzz of an almost monstrous fecundity at Tinker Creek, is reproduced in every ecological niche.[1] Nature is not the tame workshop of the nineteenth century's picturing but an explosive field of life that issues forth billions of new creatures, moves by the unimaginable forces of nuclear explosions and yawning black holes. Cosmic history may seem slow to us tiny onlookers, who only witness a millisecond of the universal day.

In itself cosmic history is constant change, as continents shift, stars recede, mountains thrust to the skies. On the cosmic scale the rule of being and life is as Buddhism's three marks picture it: painful, fleeting, and selfless—above all fleeting.

But nature or the cosmos is not something outside us. We are something inside it, parts of the cosmic whole. Our cells obey biochemical laws. Our bodies are bound by gravity. We take life from earlier instances of our species, pass that life along to our successors, and finally return to the Great Clod that receives all the bodies that tramp it. Consequently, we must make religious, ultimate sense of nature, working out its place in our scheme of things. Like our friends, our family members, our enemies, our bodies, our selves, nature begs correlation with the love at the center of our faith.

In the case of children, nature can seem a kaleidoscope of colors and sounds and smells. Through our middle years, most of us modern Westerners mainly think of nature as a source of raw materials. But in our later years, when there is an inclination to think things in the round, the weather and the garden can become soothing, instructive, a strong ingredient in the love of wisdom that makes for artful dying. Then it is clear that the world of God is much vaster than the world of our doings, our friends, our powers of thought. God is doing things, diffusing divine love, in places and forms, colors and harmonies, we shall never be aware of. When our souls open to praise this creativity, our hearts acknowledge the connections implicit in our blood, we gain a crucial sense of proportion, a wonderful expansion of faith. "All this God has loved into being," we murmur, "and I have been privileged to take part."

Creation

For many East Asian peoples, what we think of as the impersonal side of divinity, God as a force rather than a knowing subject, has virtually coincided with nature. Thus the Chinese Tao or Way that moves the ten thousand things of creation treats them all like straw dogs: impersonally and unemotionally. If a baby and a chair lie in the path of an onrushing flood, both will be swept away. If a drought afflicts a province, both its animals and its humans will suffer. Not separating the sacred from the natural, East Asia, and most non-literate cultures, strove to harmonize themselves with the way things simply were. Things were both regular and unpredictable, both seasonal and never assured. So wisdom was moving lightly, responsively, in keeping with nature's present flow. Good rule among human beings was an active not-doing *(wu-wei)*, a persuasion rather than a power-play. For the Tao held sway like a woman—indirectly, and like a baby—through apparent powerlessness. As water wears away stone, so the Tao did its work patiently, steadily, confounding superficial judgments of strength.

In trying to attune themselves to nature's Way, most East Asians inculcated a certain holism. Many Japanese Buddhists, for example, came to picture nature's unthinking growth as superior to human beings' conflicted strivings. A cherry tree, for instance, goes into the ground as a seed, rises as a sapling, and before long flowers in exquisite blossoms. It has no adolescent identity crisis, no depressions at the climacteric. The work of nature in life-cycle matters is much more efficient than the work of us human beings, who dissipate ergs and ergs on self-doubts, false starts, reconsiderations. Nature does not have to become what it is. For nature to be is to be oneself.

Now, these views of nature, which predominated through most of pre-modern civilization, may be naive by today's scientific standards, but they provide us an important orientation. One of the major reasons we Westerners have been able to exploit nature to the point of ecological crisis is our not having respected nature as an equal, even a superior. Helped in part by the Genesis picture of human superiority, we have not shrunk from tearing the bosom of our mother with a plow, as many American Indians would have. Indeed, we have gone on to foul the waters, turn the skies caustic, erode staggering amounts of prime land. Through the centuries of Western industrialization, the great captains felt little let or hindrance from a nature conceived to be inviolable, sacred, a face and presence of God. Romantics might cast apostrophes to far mountains or near copses; peasants might know in their bones that the city's fumes were lethal; but in the boardrooms of power blackening the skies and staining the streams were almost badges of honor, trophies of human energy and will. God was so far from heaven that one could block out the sun with smog.

Today we know better, and with this knowledge should come a new theology of nature.[2] Central to such a new theology will be a retrieval of the wonder at creation that many traditional theologians exhibited. Thomas Aquinas, for example, took the metaphyics of Aristotle beyond a focus on substance or form to rivet his new system onto being *(esse)*, the act of existing or stepping forth from nothingness. Philosophizing over Exodus 3:14, where Yahweh can be translated as having named himself "I am who am," Thomas and others of his persuasion conceived God to be the font of existence, present wherever anything is. For all of creation, Augustine's personalist appreciation held good: God is more intimate to us than we are to ourselves. If we human beings are God's images, able to know and love, other creatures are yet God's vestiges, footprints of the divine Creator. For vestiges as well as images, God must not only fling the divine "let there be" against the forces of nothingness. He must continue to diffuse his being, conserving his creatures moment by moment, concurring in all their actions.

The point is the omnipresence of the Creator. Wherever anything is, lives, moves, has being, God has to be at hand. The impersonal, simply forceful side of God is the utmost ecological web. If we flee to the highest heavens, the divine light is the ultimate measuring rod. If we descend to the lowest depths, God is the fathomless bottom. The thousand who fall at our right side, like the thousand who stand at our left, all depend on God's gravity. The systole and diastole of any heart tell us chapters of God's story. If the first question is why there is something rather than nothing, creation remains aboriginal. To grasp the significance of any of our doings, we must factor the foundation of all that occurs. In Dante's phrase, God is the love that moves the stars. In Paul's intuition, in him we live and move and have our being. He is the comprehensive and we are the partial. He is the cause and we are the effect.

Thus we come to the claustrophobia of secularism. Where native religion kept the sky open, almost to the point of psychic distress, modern critical thought has set a slate roof against transcendence, for reasons less good than bad. To purchase our power to control nature, we have forfeited an open soul. Still, there are now good grounds for hope. In the growing movement to regain harmony with nature, recontact nature's sacral powers, many post-modern personalities are feeling their way back to reverencing the world as a whole.[3]

Nature's Rights

When we place the impersonal, natural side of divinity to the fore, the rights of the non-human participants in the earth's comprehensive ecology gain a significant boost. Though all creation may not have the dignity of a rational soul that images God, yet "the creation itself will be set free from its bondage to decay and obtain the glorious liberty of the children of God" (Rom 8:21). With such a destiny, creation certainly has rights over against us human beings. We cannot rape and pillage nature as we wish. The presence of God in nature's being and yearning shouts that nature is not to be abused. We did not set the stars in their patterns, give the acorns their genetic codings, paint the stripes across the zebras. Therefore, we do not have the right to destroy any of these species of creation. Use them we may, for our survival depends upon certain uses. Destroy them or seriously injure them we may not.

Another way of putting this is to say that the biblical notion of creation chastens the biblical anthropocentricity, in such wise that human beings' lordship over creation is actually a stewardship, maybe even a ministry. The biblical doctrine of creation categorically asserts that God alone is the maker of the heavens and the earth. Thus when Job rose up on his hind legs to try to bring God into court, the voice from the whirlwind stuck it right to him: "Where were you when I laid the foundation of the earth?" (Job 38:4). In this context, Adam's naming of the animals, and Adam and Eve's obligation to fill the earth and subdue it, amount to only a quite restrained hegemony. Neither the earth nor the animals are the slaves of humanity, creatures to be disposed of without a second thought. Both the animals and the earth are fellow creatures, fellow agents in the work that Teilhard de Chardin called "cosmogenesis," the becoming of the ordered whole that God began. At the least, human beings have a responsibility to husband the earth's resources. If they extend the example of their master, who came not for dominion but for service, Christians will hear a call to minister to their fellow creatures, look out for their best interests, help them to prosper handsomely.

"This is so much loose poetry," some of you may be saying. "I am not interested in wicca rites of kissing trees." Fair enough, but you have to be interested in the implications of our God-given creation, under penalty of forfeiting your Christian membership card. In the Christian view of things, human beings must fit themselves to a plan, an order, that is both bigger than themselves and not of their own making. True, human beings have great responsibilities for cosmic history, since so much of nature as well as humanity now is shaped by our politics and technology. But we cannot fulfill such responsibilities adequately without fitting ourselves to the Mystery that frames all our judgments and choices. Without a reverence for the unknowable origin of the cosmos' unknowable term, human politics and technology fall out of kilter, as manifestly they recently have done. Not thinking of themselves as but part of the *dramatis personae*, the actors of the total comedy, our modern movers and shakers have been deaf to the protests of nature that we were polluting it, blind to the collision course their greed had set. In the matter of energy consumption alone the economics of unlimited growth probably should have been seen to be absurd at least two decades ago.

The upshot for a holistic spirituality rooted in the love of God the Creator is a counter-cultural assertion of nature's strict rights. Lawyers can work out how this should influence our secular codes. Theologians might reform the old ethics and preaching, which has been a significant part of the ecological problem. In the future, the people who sit in Christian pews must see that any pollution, defacement, major injury or other abuse of nature

seriously saddens our Creator. In terms of the fifth commandment, we cannot kill the habitat, the matrix, on which we all
depend for life. The ultimate horror in nuclear war, for instance,
is not the extermination of millions of human beings. Heinous
as that would be, the still worse possibility is the destruction of
the whole biosphere. Casting aside our self-centeredness, our
immature assumption that we humans are the center of everything cosmic, we can start to take responsibility for our incursions into nature, backing away when we are not morally certain
we will not do serious harm.

Nature's Religious Gifts

When people respect nature's rights, treating the birds and
the flowers as fellow-citizens of the one cosmos, they usually
receive back some wonderful gifts. The fact that the people who
usually receive the best gifts, the most beautiful revelations, are
called "primitive" by many of our classifiers only reflects badly
on much of our classification.

Consider, for example, the aged Pygmy Moke, one of the
anthropologist Colin Turnbull's best sources of information
about the BaMbuti who live in the Congo forest:

> Normally everthing goes well in our world. But at night when
> we are sleeping, sometimes things go wrong, because we are
> not awake to stop them from going wrong. Army ants invade
> the camp; leopards may come in and steal a hunting dog or
> even a child. If we were awake these things would not happen.
> So when something big goes wrong, like illness or bad hunting
> or death, it must be because the forest is sleeping and not look-
> ing after its children. So what do we do? We wake it up. We
> wake it up by singing to it, and we do this because we want it
> to awaken happy. Then everything will be well and good
> again. So when our world is going well then also we sing to
> the forest because we want it to share our happiness.[4]

I wonder how many of us "developed" people have a view
of the world so beautiful. For Moke the forest is the near, parental face of divinity, as his later statements make fully clear. The

forest gives the Pygmies so many good things that Moke is sure
its stable disposition is benevolent. Only by accident does mis-
fortune or sadness enter in. Therefore Moke's people try to treat
the forest kindly, gratefully, singing to make it feel good. They
try to treat the forest the way they themselves like to be treated,
with consideration and love.

The application to our own situation is easy to make. We,
too, should try to treat nature the way we ourselves like to be
treated. In our case, as much as the Pygmies', the golden rule
should apply. Has not nature provided us our food and drink,
our sun and rain? Are not the evils that twist our lives into pain
much more the product of human greed and cruelty than the
product of nature's destructive power? If we see nature aright, it
is ever on the verge of giving us good things: food and shelter,
work for our minds and elevation for our spirits. Whenever we
wish, this bounty can make nature the forceful presence of God.
As Turnbull reports another of Moke's explanations:

> He told me how all Pygmies have different names for their god,
> but how they all know that it is really the same one. Just what
> it is, of course, they don't know, and that is why the name
> really does not matter very much. "How can we know?" he
> asked. "We can't see him; perhaps only when we die will we
> know and then we can't tell anyone. So how can we say what
> he is like or what his name is? But he must be good to give us
> so many things. He must be of the forest. So when we sing, we
> sing to the forest."[5]

In Moke's case, a serene peace seems to fill the space
between informant and questioner. The forest is a stable zone of
good will, the Pygmies' unquestioned home. Among other subjects of his study, such as the Ik, a tribe displaced from their traditional hunting routes along the border between northern
Kenya and Uganda, Turnbull found nature to be hostile, unsup-
portive, the crumbled linch-pin of a world that had fallen apart.[6]
We cannot say categorically, therefore, that all non-literate people, all throwbacks to the age of paleolithic hunting and gathering, find nature bountiful and kind. Still, the Ik are almost the

exception that proves the general rule. The dislocations in their habitat were man-made, not natural. It was due to human bungling, not nature's caprice, that their age-old patterns were disrupted, and with these patterns their sense of orientation, their surety of meaning. Left to themselves, not made pawns in an emerging nations' power-game, the Ik probably would continue to gaze with awe and gratitude upon Mount Morungole:

> From the *di* [sitting place], Morungole looked immense. I asked about going to the top, and there was no objection, but I sensed that I had asked the wrong question. Then Lemu, a Dodos *moran* [initiated warrior], took his spear and pointed to a dark, rich streak running almost vertically, it seemed, up and down the side of the mountain. He said, "That is a good place." The others just nodded. Lemu added, "That is the Place of God." And again the others just nodded.[7]

The place of God organizes the traditional person's world. The splendor of God shining forth in the sky or on the waters is the center of the traditional person's universe. C. G. Jung found this dramatically true in the case of Ochwiay Biano, a Pueblo Indian of the American southwest:

> Their religious conceptions are not theories to them (which, indeed, would have to be very curious theories to evoke tears from a man), but facts, as important and moving as the corresponding external realities. As I sat with Ochwiay Biano on the roof, the blazing sun rising higher and higher, he said, pointing to the sun, "Is not he who moves there our father? How can anyone say differently? How can there be another god? Nothing can be without the sun." His excitement, which was already perceptible mounted still higher; he struggled for words, and exclaimed, at last, "What would a man do alone in the mountains? He cannot even build his fire without him."[8]

Perhaps nature's best gift is to remind us of our neediness, and so offer us strong assurances that we are not alone.

Chapter Three
Economics

The Marxist Insight

To set nature in a Christian framework, we tried to show the connections among all of God's creatures, the propriety of considering them all spokes pointing back to the divine love. In our own lives of faith, nature's rights and religious gifts seemed to stand as candidates for a love relation, to provide the basis for a golden treatment of nature as we ourselves wish to be treated. Much the same set of dispositions should obtain in the realm of economics, our next consideration. As much as nature, or any other significant domain of our lives, economics begs correlation with the center of our faith, the unearthly love of God. If we are not to be schizophrenic but whole, we must get a proper fix on our money and banking, make sure that we run them and not they us. Otherwise we will be out of phase with Jesus' kingdom, alienated from good order and health.

Among the economic theories on the current world scene, Marxism has laid the greatest stress on alienation. To be sure, the totalitarian regimes that owe some philosophical debt to Marx alienate their own citizens egregiously, but the classical theories of Marx himself were much more humanistic.[1] In large measure, they were an effort to bridge the gap between nature and human beings that the industrial revolution had created. Whereas at times past most people had enjoyed a work that was somewhat fulfilling, somewhat amenable to the imprint of their own individual craft, in the wake of the industrial revolution labor had become alienated, cut away from the worker like a dismembered limb. The moment that machines became more efficient than human beings, the big owners would throw human beings on the scrap heap. It is hard in a time such as that in which I am writing, when unemployment has reached double-digits, not to find Marx's basic outlook considerably verified. Without accepting the atheism that has helped many Marxists to trample on human rights, we could use Marx to rethink our social ethics.

What, then, would a humanistic Marxist have work and economics become? What correlation could there be between the holistic aspirations of a representative Christian spirituality and a Marxist regime of liberation? A humanistic Marxist, one who tried to appropriate Marx's deep insights into the overall contribution that good work could make, would have work and economics become harmonizing rather than alienating, servant of the common good rather than servant of the privileged few. In that way, such a person would be at least cousin to the biblical Christian, who knows that it is easier for a camel to pass through the eye of a needle than for a rich person to enter the kingdom of God because so many rich people take their profits from the aches and tears of their fellow human beings. Marx saw that work, which should have been a person's noble vocation, the way both of developing the self and serving the commonweal, instead had become a bed of pain, a grimy mercantile rack. In an age that lacked child labor laws, that gave little protection even to nursing women, Marx's contemporaries saw so ugly a face atop the factory chimneys that they felt Satan was flying high. Under the convenient guise of the rights of capital, Satan was grinding all sorts of people down. Marx and his fellow disaffected economists knew there had to be a better way to do business.

It seems to me that E. F. Schumacher, the late British economist, retained the best of Marx's insights, and brought them even more clearly in line with religious intuition, when he wrote his famous essay on a Buddhist way to do business. In con-

trast to the West's view of work, which tends to be unanalyzed
and left to the whim of the marketplace, he asserted:

> The Buddhist point of view takes the function of work to be at
> least three-fold: to give a man a chance to utilise and develop
> his faculties; to enable him to overcome his ego-centredness by
> joining with other people in a common task; and to bring forth
> the goods and services needed for a becoming existence. . . . To
> organize work in such a manner that it becomes meaningless,
> boring, stultifying, or nerve-wracking for the worker would be
> little short of criminal; it would indicate a greater concern with
> goods than with people, an evil lack of compassion and a soul-
> destroying degree of attachment to the most primitive side of
> this worldly existence.[2]

As Robert L. Heilbroner has shown, Marx came to see commodities as telltale clues to a society's system of values.[3] In its
trail of commodities a society left a story of how it stratified its
classes, how it correlated its money and labor, what it did with
the largest amount of its citizens' lifetime: their years of work.
We do not have to accept Marx's shallow atheism or materialistic
philosophy of history to applaud his perception in fixing his
gaze on the instruments of a society's production. Where most
philosophers rushed past the significance of the assembly lines
and furnaces, consigning them to the business pages, Marx saw
that the way our places of work tie together our social interactions, creativity, ideological constructs, and the like makes them
the very key to our cultures' meanings. Family life, politics, art,
and even religion turn out to be different in an industrial age
than they were in an agrarian age. You cannot alienate labor in
any significant degree and have a social body that is healthy and
whole. For that reason, spiritual theologians have a special obligation to inform themselves about Marx.

Christian Labor

From the New Testament to such recent expressions of
Christian labor theory as Pope John Paul II's encyclical *Laborem
Exercens*, Christian theologians have striven to present a balanced

view of human work, one that would do justice to all the data in the central tradition and the several sides of the work experience itself. So traditionally one has found developments of the Genesis doctrine that human beings are to subdue the earth, making it bear fruit, the Genesis doctrine that men are to earn their bread by the sweat of their brow and women are to earn their redemption by childbearing, and the New Testament doctrine that the laborer is worthy of his hire. Similarly, traditional theologians have stressed that the goods of the earth exist for all the earth's people, that justice and fair-dealing are all people's due, and that the way we treat one another will have a major say in how God treats us. Looking at the experience of the farmer, the Christian theoreticians could see many advantages in a life close to the soil. Looking at the experience of the artisan, they could see close similarities to the divine creation. In any decent work, human beings could offer their labors to God, feeling both that they were paying their own way and that they were easing some of the debt they carried as sinners. In any dubious work, such as serving in the military or lending money, theologians tried to accent the positive and minimize the negative: soldiers were to try to contain their depredations and serve only just causes; bankers were to bend over backward not to let money take precedence over human welfare.

We shall have full occasion to pursue some of these collateral issues that any consideration of labor is bound to raise, but our main focus here is an explicitly Christian view of the time and energy we spend at work. It seems to me that we could do far worse than try to build on Freud's dictum that good mental health involves the ability to love and to work. Focusing on the ability to work we can ask, "How does the time I spend at 'work' shape the self I bring to God and my neighbors, shape the society in the midst of which I share a providential time?" For Christians, good mental health is not so much accommodation to the average mores of their society as harmony with Jesus' twofold command. The balance and creativity we seek from work is one that finally stems from the infusions of the Spirit, who works to heal and perfect us. Not that the Spirit's movements contradict the findings of sound psychology. Almost always they occur in and through our ordinary psychodynamics, not against their grain. But the Spirit's movements make it clearer than many psychoanalytic theories seem to do that love is the wellspring of all creativity, in human relations and work alike, and that where there is real charity and love God truly abides in our midst.

For the personal side of a Christian labor theory, we might stress freshness and service. People who make things that are new, original, or beautiful have a special vocation. They may be artists, scientists, parents, theologians, administrators—the field does not matter. What matters is a newness of vision, a fresh way of combining old pieces, a capacity for shaking us out of our ruts and bringing the world back to life. A good measure of the health of a society's economy is the value it puts on such people. If art and science, creative parenting and medicine, music and theology rank high, an economy shows good signs that it really is a system serving the general populace, a flow of goods and services mindful of its people's soul. The same with the value a society puts on its service sector. What sort of rewards, financial and emotional, do a society's teachers, nurses, social workers, and child-care personnel receive? Who says a good word, gives a good check, to the dedicated corps that make its public bureaucracies go?

For the social side of a Christian labor theory, I would stress the vocations that provide the most central services, and the vocations that are prophetic, geared to keeping the whole people mindful of their reason to be. The most central services clearly are food production, the provision of shelter and clothing, the provision of education and medicine, and the provision of a legitimate group defense. Beyond these services, a particular kind of work should have to pass close scrutiny, since its apparently unessential nature ought to cause us to require special evidence of its decency or utility. Jesus said it once and for all: We cannot serve God and mammon.

The prophetic vocations are those countercultural works that deliberately go against the stream in order to remind the populace at large that it profits none of us to gain the whole world and suffer the loss of our immortal soul. The prophetic vocation can surface in many garbs, especially in such a polyvocal time as our own. However, one expects the churches and universities to be prophetic almost full-time, so it is the churches and universities that have a special obligation to concretize a Christian labor theory.

Money

At the core of the economic order is money, capital and profit. Both have a decent connotation, but both ring ominously in religious ears. Money is too closely connected with mammon, the spirit of this-worldly prosperity, for it not to stiffen the visage of most religions' saints. Christian anchorites, Muslim sufis, and Jewish hasidim all tend to appear in tattered robes, rather than fine silks and linens. Buddhist and Hindu holy men traditionally have supported themselves by begging. For the followers of Jesus, the Master's tribute to John the Baptist will always thrust a stake into mammon's heart: "What did you go out into the wilderness to behold? A reed shaken by the wind? Why then did you go out? To see a man clothed in soft raiment? Behold, those who wear soft raiment are in kings' houses. Why then did you go out? To see a prophet? Yes, I tell you, and more than a prophet" (Mt 11:7–9). John did not gain his status by money.

This is not a lesson most of us learn easily. When Popes feel they must comport themselves like princes, the natural human resistance to Jesus' plain meaning stands clear. Most religious orders have vowed poverty as part of their ascetical ideal, but only a small fraction of monks and nuns have ever shared the anxieties of the truly poor, those for whom daily bread is a sign of the Father's direct care. We compromise, most of us, struggling to get money in perspective. We need it to live and move, if not to have our being, yet we fear its growing tentacles, the ease with which it wraps us round. Unless we are reflective, self-disciplining, we keep upping the ante of our strivings. First we need more room, then better furniture, then a full landscaping, then a new car. When orthodontia and ballet lessons are at hand, membership in the country club cannot be far behind.

The Confucians tended to think of the life-cycle in terms of three major struggles that a (male) person had to carry out successfully. In young adulthood the problem was lust. In maturity the problem was strife. In old age the problem was greed.[4] It would seem that these struggles remain with us yet. Perhaps because of the onset of physical decline, with its increased sense of vulnerability, the older generation appears to cling to things, become preoccupied with stocks and securities, drift toward the right in politics and social conscience. Naturally this is no hard and fast rule. There are neo-conservatives scarcely out of their twenties, acquisitive monomaniacs in every group of the middle-aged. Equally, there are splendid specimens of older maturity, in whom generosity and compassion fully rule the day. But, by and large, the Chinese stereotype bears reflection. Consider the angry red faces of the government employees, both civilian and military, who find their "double-dipping" threatened. Consider the plight of states such as Kansas, where taxes have not kept pace with inflation because the desires of the older wealthy have prevailed over the needs of the younger poor.

Yes, money is a big problem, an item hard to love well. Sensing this, most of the this-worldly traditions have tried to counter-balance their approval of wealth with strong social responsibilities. Thus Judaism, which is not an ascetic tradition, has expected its fortunate citizens to contribute generously to the community coffers. Thus Islam, also not an ascetic tradition, has sponsored the *zakat* or alms. Christianity, however, is an ascetic religion, if Jesus be its central exemplar. To let the splendor of the incarnation blaze forth, Jesus chose a life in which his food and drink were his Father's will, he did not raise his own family, he was one of the people who had no place to lay his head. The incarnationalism, sacramentality, and iconography that the Christian doctrines of creation and grace must always sponsor stand in tension with the stripping, need for sacrificial choice, and sense of the Spirit's superiority to flesh that hew equally close to the Christian mainline. In the best of times, this tension makes a crackling electricity, a cadre of followers fully alive. In the majority of times since Constantine's establishment of Christianity as a protected religion, the tension has slackened and Jesus' followers have scrambled to pile up things. The contemporary garage sale bears a sobering resemblance to the Byzantine bazaar.

In the age of the bazaar, one will not love money well without struggling. Following Jesus on this point means saying no to the general drift of American culture at large. Much of the trick lies in making Paul's battle-cry a personal anthem: "For freedom Christ has set us free!" Freed by Christ, are we going to enslave ourselves to patios and stock portfolios? Set loose from this-worldly concerns, are we going to preoccupy ourselves with insurance and banking? Not if we take so little as fifteen minutes a day to study the evangelical Christ. He did not serve God and mammon. He did not love well-stocked barns or bars. Jesus would not have made a good Rotarian. I doubt that he would have sold bonds for Israel. Those were not the things that mattered. The things that mattered were love of God and love of neighbor, moving through the world lightly, keeping one's eye upon the goal, following the master when the road forked toward scandal, not averting one's face even when there came the cross. People who embrace this sort of program have little time to care about money. For healthy Christians money is at most a significant means, part of God's hundredfold.

Are there not, however, more positive injunctions about money? Can one not give wealthy or moderately wealthy Christians better indications of what they might do with their wealth? One can, of course. For example, there is the traditional virtue of almsgiving, which never goes out of style. As it is pious and useful to pray for the dead, so it is pious (in the best sense) and useful to give aid to those in need. With or without a formal tithe, many Christians are very generous in almsgiving. Most of our schools, hospitals, and other places of succor owe the generosity of the wealthy a great deal. In quiet ways, as though their left hand did not know what their right hand was doing, the best of these benefactors pile up a rich reward from their heavenly Father, who sees their secret good works and contrives to prepare them a full recompense.

Private almsgiving never goes out of style, even in a time like our own, when the limits of its individualistic orientation have started to show. For today, in addition to direct aid to suf-

fering individuals, we do well to put our time, and probably
much of our money, toward the repair of dysfunctional *systems*.
The cracks in our health care system, social security system,
unemployment compensation, and the like show some of the
many ways in which our country's suffering people are not
receiving the aid that most of us want them to have. In parallel
fashion, the bigger cracks in the worldwide systems of food distribution, health care, education, and the like suggest that
wealthy people might resolve to target international relief agencies and the reform of international politics. I suspect that this
kind of generosity may prove to be the next generation's way to
the biblical good measure, pressed down and overflowing.

Conservation

As Christian instinct shies away from acquisitiveness, so it
shies away from prodigality and waste. If the implications of
Christian faith put a hindrance before money-loving, the implications of Christian stewardship put a blue ribbon around conservation. Against the money-driven economies of unlimited
growth, the program of Jesus would call us back to simplicity
and generous sharing. That may seem a tame enough call, when
one contemplates it in the Sunday morning sunshine. Put into
the workaday world, it is a writ of economic revolution, for arm
in arm with environmentalists, it would create an army of people
with their consciousness sufficiently raised for them to realize
the brainwashing that the industrial-military complex has
effected. To power their own establishments, moguls and majors
have kept escalating their supposed need for more. It is time for
the prophets among us to point out that these emperors have no
clothes.

You can find the relevant figures on conservation in any
good college textbook.[5] They make it clear that the "energy crisis" is mainly a matter of our inefficiency and ersatz needs. We
have more than enough energy, if the goal is supplying the
power to care for society's essential needs. The supplement
needed for a quite comfortable life lies ready to hand in solar and

other natural sources, if we have the will to develop it. A person I know who just built a solar house expects to get two-thirds to three-fourths of his heating from a simple sun-space. Since the electrical system he must join is one of those many with a nuclear white elephant on its hands, these fractions will mean hundreds of dollars saved each year. Yet the people building the huge general activities building at the university near this man's house turned their noses up at using solar energy. Hundreds of thousands of dollars that might have gone for books and faculty now will go into heating a swimming pool. Is that another case of simple stupidity, or another case of careful collusion? What a burden that we have to ask this question so often.

In an economy compatible with Christian instincts, things would be used carefully. The space necessary for beauty would so often dovetail with simplicity that art and efficiency would be sisters. Like a new thought borrowed from pre-historic humanity, human beings would again have a care for posterity. Taking the giant winch of imagination, a sizable number of people actually would begin to try to picture the needs of the year 2100. Of course they would have to pay a good price. The figures on resource depletion would no longer be merely academic. In consequence, preserving what we currently possess, moving to a renewable resource base, and starting to see the beauty of small systems would step forth as speedy entailments. But the major contribution of a Christian set of economic instincts would not be even this sprightly imagination, since, after all, we have had steady-state economists and persuasive conservationists for well-neigh a solid generation. The major contribution of a Christian set of economic instincts would be the will to start enacting some of the splendid scenarios that the pioneer imaginers have developed.

As a tribute to such giants as E. F. Schumacher and Barbara Ward, let us meditate on this summoning of will power. Were it serious, it would begin to put its money where its vision lay. That would mean supporting steady-state, conservationist policies in energy production, home-building, transportation design, agriculture, and a dozen other areas. It would mean standing against planned obsolescence, bad craftsmanship, an economy built on chemicals. In a minor capacity, it would deal another body-blow to the military establishment, which is egregiously wasteful as well as egregiously lethal. In a major capacity, it would mount a campaign for quality, competence, and efficiency. Moral theologians would begin to think again about sins of slovenliness. Religious ethicians would again take aim at greed. Joined to lobbyists for distributive justice, Christians would feel themselves the front-wave of a new social order, an old reverence for life. Most of us have only the barest notion of how good this could feel.

As the spiritual life teaches all who take it seriously that dying and living are paradoxical, so it teaches even beginners that less can be very much more. With less clutter in our cellars, we can make a family room. With less clutter in our minds, we can have an original thought. Good things happen in family rooms, things of quality and spirit. Good things happen in uncluttered minds, things called science, art, and innovation. Most of us now have so much junk, and so little spiritual mobility, that we are like pack horses, bent and shackled. Spring and fall, we throw out thrice-worn clothes, but only to make room for something novel. Even in times of supposed recession, the amounts we waste are staggering. If we halved our possessions and halved our errands our quality of life would likely double. But for fear of space, spiritual agrophobia, we keep up the constant rotation. Yet an ironclad law says that we cannot fudge the exercises the Spirit requires of us, that we must have unencumbered spirits.

So, to be whole, we must come at economics along what will initially seem a tangent. Spending time with Jesus and his marginal friends, we will find that the affluent main streets no longer feel comfortable. Then, if we sluice off to the side-roads, we can collect in helpful pools. There, if we are fortunate, we can start to suspect what a poor church could really be.

Essentially, a poor church could be a place where people sat down together and seriously considered pooling their money. Taking their fellowship in Christ as something utterly real, they could try to make sure that no one lacked necessities while someone else enjoyed luxuries. The spirit of this reflection and effort to share would not be bitter or pressured. The spirit would be gentle and cooperative. Seeing you, my brother in need, how can I close my heart against you? Finding that you, my sister in faith, are suffering great fear and want, how can I not reach out to help? What I am able to do will vary with my own circumstances, but often it will help a great deal. Indeed, just the fact that I am willing to *try* to share your pain, consider your plight something that pertains to me, will undercut a large part of your misery. For by convincing you that you are not alone, and that your economic troubles are not something for which you should feel guilty, I can put new life into the faith of both of us. In this way, sharing their real troubles and joys, Christians have made genuine churches for centuries, often conquering the worst of times.

Chapter Four
Politics

The Common Good

The central notion of any healthy politics, the common good, links conservation with politics, by underscoring our obligation to preserve the first "commons," the natural environment. Seriously to injure or wantonly diminish the natural environment would be to slash at the matrix of future generations' livelihood. Only the most selfish, arrogant, or shortsighted groups would be willing to defend such policies, were we to drag our common business out into the noonday light. But many people are willing to proceed according to such policies, as long as they can do business in smoky back rooms. As the Gospel of John put it long ago: "Every one who does evil hates the light, and does not come to the light, lest his deeds should be exposed" (3:20). The first requisite for a healthy politics, one that would be compatible with Christian faith, is that it take place in the light, adhere to a pervasive set of sunshine laws.

More important even than sunshine laws, however, is the underlying motivation of a community's politicians. Unless they have a sincere desire to do business honestly, politicians will circumvent the most ideal sunshine laws. And they will only have a sincere desire to do business honestly if they are convinced that honest dealing is itself a central pillar of the common good. As long as the partners to any social enterprise think that "society" is something other than the common good that might appear, were people to live together honestly and lovingly, their social enterprise is bound to wander in debilitating darkness. If a blind man leads a blind man, both fall in a ditch.

I am saying, then, that the central path to the common good, the central goal of a decent human politics, is doing business in the light. With such a center, one has all the orientation that a holistic Christian spirituality needs, if it is to make politics a zone it can love, a dimension of human thinking and doing that need not blush before God. The common good does not reside in money, material products, or the strange amalgam of the two called the "Gross National Product." We do not find the common good by consulting the Dow Jones or the Index of Leading Economic Indicators. The common good is people living together openly and supportively, sharing goods and trials equally.

When danger arises, people rightly oriented toward the common good band together, dividing their burdens and fears. When good harvests roll in, people rightly oriented toward the common good celebrate generously, with a single spirit of gratitude and joy. Although they need owe no allegiance to Marx, such people instinctively embody the Marxist dictum of giving to each according to his or her need and taking from each according to his or her productive ability. In Christian parlance, they hold all things in common, due to their bonds of love.

Now and then one sees such a community. In an extended family, a small church, or a pre-literate tribe, the common good can actually hold center stage, actually be clearly viable. Probably such pockets of human perfection have always been rare, but their symbolic significance far outweighs their rare occurrence. For they model the most important lesson in any social undertaking, the lesson we are all most in danger of forgetting. This is the evangelical political science: we will know the quality of any undertaking by its fruits; the nature of human beings becomes manifest in what they do. So a church that trumpets about justice but leaves its female members disenfranchised is obviously not authoritative. So a country that allows a few people to wax fat while a great many grow thin with despair is obviously in need of reform.

Underneath these judgments, however, is the corollary that things need not be this way. The disparity in human beings' fruits—the few places of lightsome politics and many places of dim—says that the kind of communities we build are very much our own doing. We could have a fair sharing of the goods of the earth, if we wished. We could divide the benefits and suffer the pains quite equally. To do so we need only recall the way that Jesus included all people in his outreach, replaced "mine" and "thine" with "ours." Completely identifying his cause with our own, Jesus fashioned a mystical body. Reflecting the unifying love of his God, Jesus joined himself to his followers like a vine to its branches.

Distributive Justice

Distributive justice is the equity or fairness that should prevail in the distribution of a society's goods. Taking a given number of people as a system, one can analyze how they tend to share in the money, power, services, and other goods that flow back and forth among them. The only fully adequate system is the international whole of us, so interrelated have our economies and political units become, but it still makes sense to analyze how a given country distributes its wealth, how a given state divides up its tax burdens, who does and does not benefit from the social services of a given county. If the analysis is not merely a matter of curiosity, the point will be to search out the patterns that seem to be unjust and favor some citizens at the expense of others. Under the assumption that the goods of the earth are for all the earth's people (an assumption that the Christian doctrine of creation seems to make mandatory for all followers of Jesus), favoring some citizens at the expense of others will appear as an ugly blip on justice's screen. "We'll have to try to change that," conscientious politicians would say. "That simply isn't right."

The advantage of honest statistics is that they can tip us off to major patterns that simply are not right. For example, the current economic pattern in which the dollars of working men balance at fifty-nine cents for working women shouts of sexual injustice. So great a disparity in the sexes' share in the monetary rewards of work simply should not be—if men and women are indeed essentially equal. The same with the current statistics on black and white unemployment. If white unemployment is significantly less than black—say, eight to sixteen percent—then the provisions of the American Constitution and the Christian Church both stand roundly mocked. Turning the anger that such statistics should produce to positive account, we could try to praise and aid the places—factories, offices, and employment agencies—that have developed new ways to work. Stressing flextime, shared jobs, and workers' sharing in economic decisions, we could encourage all those who try to make work the right and privilege of each of us, the important source of dignity that the Popes' social encyclicals increasingly have stressed.

This could apply in all towns, all states, all countries. If the counties of Northern Ireland were to strive for economic and political patterns that put Catholics on a par with Protestants, the religious hatreds between these two groups would be almost sure to improve. First let there be equal secular citizenship. Then we will see how intractable the religious bigotries really are. Parallel intuitions present themselves in the cases of Lebanon and Israel. If the Muslims and Christians of Lebanon were really to try to share their country's political and economic goods fairly, their age-old ethnic and religious differences would have a chance of settling to manageable proportions. If the Jews of Israel began to treat the Arabs of Israel as economic and political equals, fellow title-holders to the holy land, they might find good prospects for lasting peace.

Distributive justice therefore is a good test of a people's sincerity. The way that Jews really feel about Arabs is reflected in their laws and business statistics. The way that whites really regard blacks stands manifest in how they share the economic pie. Churches that will not admit women to political power preach social justice at their peril. Companies that support military dictatorships have little basis for outrage when their own personnel are slashed. We are not rightly judged by what we say about others but by what we do. When we work for justice, fair-dealing, and equal opportunity, we can claim to be healthy politicians. When we put our money, time, and influence at the service of increasing justice, we share the praise for justice's nearer approach.

For holistic spiritual theologians, the point is not so much organizing marches as clarifying where the focus of Christian love should fall. Until people rightly love distributive justice, are strongly drawn to the vision of radical fair-sharing, the political portion of their social life falls outside the energies of redemption. If it is inconceivable that Jesus would support a tilted access to opportunities for education, health care, good food, decent clothing, and useful work, then the follower of Jesus has to love equal access to these social goods. It does not compute to enter any different equation. And since the love that Jesus expresses is not flimsy but strong and practical, Jesus' followers' love of equal access to society's main goods ought to be the stuff of strong economic, political, and social programs.

For example, it makes little sense to claim one is a follower of Jesus, a lover of the God of light and the equal neighbor the way that Jesus was, and not expect one's country or state to have a fair tax code. To have an unfair tax code, a sharing of the common burdens that causes some to bear little onus and others to bear great, is to fly in the face of Christian social philosophy. The practical effect of such instinct, one would think, would be a concerted effort to reform one's country's tax code, close its shameless loopholes, shut down its legions of parasitic lawyers. Unless they publish news of their doings in organs that I never see, Christians have not been signal for clamoring after such tax reform. Their love of the common good, regard for the neighborly whole, has not flowed out in this holistic way. When I analyze why this should be, what state of soul it evidences, I do not find much that is exculpating. The love of money is indeed the root of great evils.

Poverty and Marginalization

Two signs that a society is not distributively just are (1) widespread disparities between the incomes of the rich and the incomes of the poor and (2) large numbers of people cut off from the society's centers of power, forced to subsist at the margins. Globally, there can be no doubt that the current situation among the whole of our race, the vast multitude of us now approaching five billion, is unjust to the point of scandal. Consider, for example, some figures on food: "There are more hungry people in the world now than there have ever been. More than 1,000 million may not get enough to meet their energy calorie requirements. And over 450 million of these, or a quarter of the population of the developing market economies, are estimated to suffer from serious undernutrition. Over 60% of them live in the most seriously affected countries, mostly in the Far East, and the majority are rural people. . . . Raising the food intake of the over 450 million severely undernourished to the level of their nutritional requirements would involve the equivalent of 40–60 million tons of wheat per year. This is not more than 3–5% of present world cereal consumption, or 10–15% of the cereals now being fed to livestock in the developed countries."[1]

Nor should we think that the canons of distributive justice only point blame across the North-South divide. Within the United States the drift in the early 1980s was away from what common sense or fair play would call justice: "The Food Stamps program serves 22 million Americans with average gross incomes of $325 a month—or $3,900 a year—and average cash assets of $66. As a result of the Reagan Administration's first round of cuts, over 1 million of these people are being removed from the program. . . . After Reagan announced his 1983 budget and tax cuts, the Congressional Budget Office estimated the effects on families at various levels of income. A family with an income of less than $10,000 per year would pay $120 less in taxes but would lose an average of $360 in federal benefits. On the other hand, households with incomes above $80,000 will pay $15,000 less in taxes and will lose $120 in federal benefits."[2]

Because of statistics such as these, which show injustice to be mottling human communities across the globe, Christian theologians have been driven back to their strongest social convictions, reinvigorating such traditions as the Roman Catholic defense of human rights. Thus David Hollenbach, at the conclusion of a study aimed at retrieving and renewing this tradition, has laid down three "strategic moral priorities": "1) The needs of the poor take priority over the wants of the rich. 2) The freedom of the dominated takes priority over the liberty of the powerful. 3) The participation of marginalized groups takes priority over the preservation of an order which excludes them."[3] One can see how implementing these strategic moral priorities would run counter to the political programs of a great many, perhaps a majority, of the world's ruling parties. If so, promulgating them is close to a sacred duty, so out of joint have the times become.

At Puebla, Mexico, the bishops of Latin America assembled for Celam III struggled with their continent's problems of poverty and marginalization. The document that their 1979 meeting produced was a consensus piece, in the main not very eloquent, but on occasion even its contemplation of the sufferings of the Latin American people led to a powerful prose: "The Church's awareness of its evangelizing mission has led it in the past ten years to publish numerous pastoral documents about social justice; to create organisms designed to express solidarity with the afflicted, to denounce outrages, and to defend human rights; to give encouragement to the option of priests and religious for the poor and the marginated; and to endure the persecution and at times death of its members in witness to its prophetic mission. Much remains to be done, of course, if the Church is to display greater oneness and solidarity. Fear of Marxism keeps many from facing up to the oppressive reality of liberal capitalism. One could say that some people, faced with the danger of one clearly sinful system, forget to denounce and combat the established reality of another equally sinful system. We must give full attention to the latter system, without overlooking the violent and atheistic historical forms of Marxism."[4]

Between the bear of liberal capitalism and the dragon of violent Marxism, the Christian politician looks for a middle way, steering not so much by ideologies as by the sight of ghetto children, the figures on how the wealth is actually shared. Where there is significant poverty, one must suspect injustice. By and large, the natural resources of most areas are sufficient to enable people to live in spare sufficiency. When nearly a quarter of the world's people are malnourished, it is time for an economic revolution. The same with the figures on people's participation in power. The very occurrence of city slums, let alone their growth through the current urbanization, is a sign that some people on the inside are taking too much, causing many people on the margins to suffer. In concert with strong planners of population control, Christians should be uniting to forge the new political systems that would target the provision of all citizens' basic needs. For this work their motto might be the old Christian tag, "No one has the right to luxuries as long as anyone lacks necessities."

Witness

There are two major modes of political action that I see as natural outlets for a Christian love of the *polis:* witness and service. In this section let us consider witness. Actually, we have been considering it all along, insofar as "witness" or testimony can take an intellectual form: proclaiming where things ought to be, and how to get there. The most dramatic forms of witness, however, occur when people do their proclaiming concretely, holistically, by putting their entire lives on the line. Vivid examples of this abound in many places. Mother Teresa of Calcutta, for example, is a "politician" of extraordinary effectiveness, through her work with the most marginal of India's poor. Catholic Worker houses in many American cities exercise a similar political ministry, reminding wealthy urbanites that thousands must live on the streets. In less obvious ways, all those who sacrifice something of their own prospects to align themselves with their society's marginals put their shoulders to the political wheel. By showing their elected leaders what is right, what government should be working to achieve, they prop at least a thin wall against the growing powers of greed.

The political witness that has struck me most powerfully is that of Stanley Rother, an American missionary priest killed in Guatemala. It happened that he visited Wichita State University, where I work, in 1981, while on a visit to his family in nearby Oklahoma. The visit had been more a flight than a vacation, since he had left hastily after learning that his name was on a right-wing hit list. His "crime" had been working, for more than ten years, with a group of poor Indians, ministering to their religious and social needs and trying to translate the New Testament into their language. He had not been "political" in the headline sense, leading marches or supporting guerrillas. In fact he had kept a low profile, wanting only to serve his people in peace. But things had come to such a pass in Guatemala that the simplest act of solidarity with the poor shamed the corrupt government. Just for being a pastor, concerned for his little flock of Guatemala's most despised, Stanley Rother was a living rebuke. So the soldiers came for him in the dead of the night (he had returned to Guatemala as soon as he thought it safe), killed him, and tried to make it look as though some of his Indians had turned against him. That is the sort of political power the United States has long countenanced in Latin America, at times directly supporting military leaders scarcely better than beasts. Stanley Rother therefore rebukes our leading politicians as well as those of Guatemala. If he is a martyr, a witness to the point of blood, the governments of Carter and Reagan are tools of a Latin American antichrist.

One could come to the same sort of conclusion by moving from Guatemala to Nicaragua. There the government of Anastasio Somoza developed a regime of gross injustice, while the little Christian community of Solentiname developed a model of political witness.[5] Once again the contrast proved more than the repressive government could bear. Somoza had his soldiers sweep down upon the Solentiname community, destroying its little chapel, dispensary, and crafts cooperative. In this case, however, there was a revolutionary movement to join. Eventually this movement (the Sandinistas) overthrew the Somoza government, and Ernesto Cardinal, the founder of the Solentiname community, came to serve the new revolutionary regime as its Minister of Culture. The end result of the Nicaraguan experiment in Christian socialism remains to be seen, but all people of good will will wish it well. If they are Americans, their main regret likely will be the alliance their country had with Somoza, and the way their country tried to thwart the justice the new regime was trying to achieve.

In the countries of Central America, opposing a brutal alliance of capitalism and militarism has led many Christians into dangerous forms of witness. Out of their conviction that right stands on the side of those fighting for change, many bishops, priests, nuns, and dedicated laity have risked their very lives. The killing of bishop Oscar Romero in El Salvador shows that the military and right wing will tolerate no voices of accusation, however well authorized. True, there is killing from the left in Latin America as well as the right, and frequently one does not know on whom to blame a given atrocity. But the left has on its side the fact that it both champions the poor and receives much of their support.

The poor, of course, would mainly like peace, and a chance to eke out a spare living. Ideology means less to them than food and clothing. Certainly there are leftists so cynical that they will afflict the poor and try to sabotage aid and reform in the name of their (in)glorious revolution. But the clearest guilt lies with the regimes of the right, often supported by North American businesses, who have blatantly served the interests of a few rich families, allowing the poor to become a great sea of misery. Witnesses in such a situation must oppose all forms of injustice, but the systemic violence of the warped status quo most of all. By turning away from its historical support of the status quo, and unleashing its prophetic energies, the Latin American church has been giving the whole world a lesson in both Christian conversion and Christian politics. Echoing Jesus' Beatitudes, it has been saying that the poor are its first constituency.

And so with many of us. Our witness may first take quite humble forms, quite undramatic ways of serving justice and peace. Not called to martyrdom, we may yet take heart from the great amount of good that we can do right where we are, at home, at work, in the local community. A large part of people's faith in human nature, their hope that political affairs actually can make a difference, depends on the way that their closest neighbors treat them. If they find justice, fair-dealing, compassion, and sensitivity in the little exchanges that make up most of their lives at work or in the neighborhood, perhaps they will be willing to hope for, and work for, justice and compassion on a larger scale. Indeed, they may even start to study the lessons of the Latin American Christian reformers, who have been spending themselves so valiantly on behalf of the poor.

Service

A second major mode of political action is service. Those who do their jobs, make their contributions to the commonweal, and keep faith with the worthwhileness of human affairs are the mainstream political influence, the force upon which society most depends.

To be sure, a great many of our mainstream servants do what they do because they think they have little choice. Not to type their pages, punch their computer keys, turn their nuts and bolts would be to join the lines of the unemployed. Then the American dream of owning their own house, driving a new car, and watching a good color television set would drift even farther away. On first glance, then, the average workers are not necessarily impressive politically. Finding some social significance in their typical stretch from 9 to 5 may require a little ingenuity.

But what else are spiritual theologians for, if not providing a little ingenuity? The trick in spiritual theology is not creating dazzling new vistas but suggesting little shifts of angle. Thus the interviews with working people that Studs Terkel has published suggest many new little wrinkles to "work." First, there is a clarification of its suffering or pathetic quality: "This book, being about work, is, by its very nature, about violence—to the spirit as well as to the body. It is about ulcers as well as accidents, about shouting matches as well as kicking the dog around. It is, above all (or beneath all), about daily humiliations. To survive the day is triumph enough for the walked wounded among the great many of us." Second, there is work's contrapuntal quality of hope: "I think most of us are looking for a calling, not a job. Most of us, like the assembly line worker, have jobs that are too small for our spirit. Jobs are not big enough for people."

The pathetic and hopeful sides of work form a dialectic, a pushing against one another that generates energy. When a laborer manages to resolve this dialectic in favor of hope, his or her work becomes a significant contribution to the common good. He or she has voted for the worthwhileness of trudging on, and so supported other workers' trudging. If Plato was correct in judging that the most important force in politics is persuasion, such supports are hard to overestimate. By deeds, which are so much more significant than words, the faithful worker offers his or her most persuasive argument: I think it is worth putting in my time. Many days, the example of one's fellow workers is all that guards one against giving up. Few indeed are the works that can stand hard scrutiny, are not well mottled by absurdity. So the hard but decent works that millions continue to perform embody immense quantities of faith and hope.

This is all the more true of works that are forthrightly servant or ministerial. Those who set their time and talent at the service of others, and do not exact a too handsome reward, are special angels of political persuasion. I know that ministering, healing, and nurturing can be very satisfying. I realize that doctors, teachers, and administrative superiors receive all sorts of strokes. But each of these professions has enough drudgery in it, enough misunderstanding and outright failure, to turn cynical a sizable fraction of its practitioners. To continue with one's spirit unsoured through a full career in any of the helping professions is no mean achievement. The mass of people one serves can be unappreciative, to say the least, and often are outright churlish. They are quick to complain and slow to pay, seldom efficient and often envious. So continuing to serve them generously, cheerfully, educes the image of Christ. Greater even than the love of one's friends is the practical love of one's clients.

What has this talk of love, service, or staying power to do with politics? How might it illumine a view of the whole? It has to do with gaining a vantage point from which all our lives càn be seen in their properly political significance. It might illumine the mutual dependence that knits us all into one body. Paul must have sometimes pondered in this vein, for consider his metaphor for Christian polity: "The body does not consist of one member but of many. If the foot should say, 'Because I am not a hand, I do not belong to the body,' that would not make it any less a part of the body. And if the ear should say, 'Because I am not an eye,

I do not belong to the body,' that would not make it any less a part of the body. If the whole body were an eye, where would be the hearing? If the whole body were an ear, where would be the sense of smell? But as it is, God arranged the organs in the body, each one of them, as he chose. If all were a single organ, where would the body be? As it is, there are many parts, yet one body. The eye cannot say to the hand, 'I have no need of you,' nor again the head to the feet, 'I have no need of you.' . . . Now you are the body of Christ, and individually members of it" (1 Cor 12:14–21. 27).

Therefore, we also serve who only do our humble jobs, merely drag our bones to their places. We serve hope: I find something to justify this day. We fulfill needs: someone waits for this bandage (lesson, brief, nursery class). True, things will not shudder to a halt if I don't show up. Yes, I am seldom indispensable. But if I quit and go down-in-the-dumps, the body will not be as lithe as it should be, the polis will not be as rich. So let me again wash another's feet, serve another's meal, break the bread and wine of my body. Is that not the Lord's example and command?

Chapter Five
Grass-Roots Communities

The Family

The love that would make us whole usually begins and ends with our families. We come from parents drawn to complement one another and in our maturity feel drawn to build our own nest. If home is the place where they always have to take you in, your familial nest is your main *Sitz im Leben,* your basic insertion into the scheme of things. For weal or woe, you carry this particular surname, have been imprinted with these particular parental visages. As long as you have a memory, your first toddling steps in the house on Oak Street or the apartment on Main will be a primordial echoing, an original orientation in life. Few pains are sharper than our regrets over a family circle prematurely broken or, worse, a family circle never formed. Few afterimages linger more consolingly than our scenes of family peace, when gods called Father and Mother stood in their heavens and all was right with a little one's world.

So the first unit of a healthy polis is the family. Whether nuclear or extended, the family is our first environment, our initial ecology. The task for a holistic Christian spirituality, then, is to help us focus our familial loves as sharply as possible, in keeping with Jesus' foci. Consider, for example, Jesus' love of his Father. Whatever his relation to Joseph, the cast of Jesus' bearing toward his heavenly Abba shows a son of astounding trust. If one of the main effects of a good parent-child relation is orienting the child so that the world is congenial, Jesus' parents did a bang-up job. Across the pages we give to history's heroes, few people have walked with Jesus' grace. Though society opposed him bitterly, because he challenged its privileged and demanded freedom of spirit, the world was yet completely comfortable, not at all an alien place.

Jesus himself therefore appears to have been a quite healthy, whole personality. From the intimate circles that first formed his character, he drew the virtues that make for depth and stability. In William James' terminology, Jesus was not a twice-born personality. He did not need to be torn down and rebuilt. True, the accounts of his "temptation" in the wilderness suggest some crisis about his vocation, but the stories of how he comported himself both before and after he burst upon the public scene suggest that any division in Jesus' psyche was at most temporary. In most of his scenes, Jesus reads his lines with such authority, such composure and peace, that his contemporaries stare at him in amazement. No one had ever spoken like him.

It pleases me to think that Jesus learned the human parts of his role in a circle of loving brothers and sisters. Whether they were technically siblings or cousins is a secondary point. To achieve the sort of psychic rootedness that Jesus exhibited, more than a good pair of parents usually is necessary. If the parents provide the foundation, and God provides the roof, there remains the question of the siding. Usually, we need good peers, supportive fellow-sharers of childhood, adolescence, maturity, and old age. Usually we need brothers, sisters, playmates, friends, colleagues. Jesus, it turned out, needed apostles and disciples. They became his second family circle.

For us today, drawing family circles that are both strong and beautiful has become quite a demanding draftmanship. On the one hand, we see myriads of houses that have ceased being homes, that might as well open themselves to boarders. The people who live there simply accept their station as a melancholy fact, a sport of evolution, and turn their attention outward. On the other hand, we see a sizable number of families that appear claustrophobic, constrained to patterns so tight they seem to walk in lockstep. Some of these claustrophobic families are very religious and even consecrate a night each week to themselves. Others are simply inbred, uncomfortable two blocks away where people pronounce three words differently. Virtue, as always, lies in the middle. The house must be open enough to be ventilated, well enough insulated to retain the warmth of the sun. If the inhabitants have too little connection, they will quickly drift apart. If they live on top of one another, they will come out runty and retarded.

All power and praise, then, to the families able to work out these delicate balances, nimble enough to negotiate these frightening high wires. One that I know is now starting its third generation, reknitting its already strong bonds in a common fascination with the first grandchild. The parents seem to have kept good contacts with their own brothers and sisters. They seem also to have fostered many friends. With their children the most striking feature is their fusion of freedom and trust. They allowed their kids to unfold their wings, never kept them on too short leashes. Yet they must also have given their kids boundaries, sufficient definition, to keep their freedom from being chaotic and too threatening properly to be utilized. "They trusted their kids into responsibility," one finally hears oneself exclaim. "By their policy of assuming the best (but not being blind to the possibility of the worst), accenting the positive (but discussing the gory headlines), they slowly became consummate initiators into reality. Like the rites of passage of archaic peoples, their interactions with their kids ushered in the divine mysteries." When a family is a place where kids grow intimate and comfortable with the divine mysteries, it is an inexhaustible font of wholeness.

Friendship

The central point of a holistic family circle is probably the friendship between the founding partners, the two spouses from whom the circle emanates. It may seem surprising to refer to marriage in this way, as a primal form of friendship, but a little reflection should make the reference quite apt. To be sure, spouses typically begin their relation in erotic attraction, wanting to be with one another through and through. Delight in the other's beauty of body and spirit is the first energy in most good marriages. But if the initial eros is to mature, become an energy of life, it must take on many of the modalities of friendship, expand to include a delight in oneness of mind. *Homonoia*, the like-mindedness at the core of the classical view of friendship, is as important for spouses as for any other friends. When spouses fall out of like-mindedness, their eros develops a gaping hole.[1]

One of the happy effects of the women's movement seems to be a spotlighting of the dynamics of marital friendship. When men and women are considered equal, the parity necessary for friendship can assert itself. Then it seems more natural for parenting to become a shared enterprise, with few of its tasks sexually determined. And then it seems more natural for spouses to share common ventures in the world of work. For example, the cooperative company building our home is anchored by a husband-wife team. He is the architect and general contractor. She is the financial officer (bookkeeper, paymaster, custodian of inventories) and interior decorator. The other members of the cooperative (all men) play designated roles as carpenters, tile layers, or framers, but the hinge is the husband-wife team. Their family life and their work overlap so thoroughly that it must be hard for them to mark where one begins and the other leaves off.

Love and work are our two main projects in life, so their fruitful connection is a great boost for holism. Today more and more households appear to prize such a connection, with interesting fringe benefits. For example, another husband and wife I know have teamed up for educational ventures focused on self-help. He is a specialist in general education, she is a professor of nursing especially interested in holistic medicine, and "self-help" has emerged as a concept central to both their studies. Initially, she saw the importance of self-help, or taking personal responsibility, in the field of health care. Depressed by the string of patients whose problems were rooted in their life-styles (bad nutrition, lack of exercise, patterns of high stress, and the like), she began to explore both preventive and holistic points of view, concentrating on the role of the patient. The analogy to education sprang to mind through the offices of one of his students. The student had gone through a modified Great Books program, and then specialized in exercise therapy. Reflecting on this career pattern, the student expressed gratitude for the demands the Great Books education had made on his personal initiative, since personal initiative had emerged as a central factor in his programs of exercise therapy. Just as he had had to take responsibility for integrating the different aspects of his general education, so he was asking his patients to take hold of programs of jogging, stretching, weight-lifting and the like designed to heal them of past injuries or simply to increase their level of health.

For this pair of spousal friends, general education and holistic medicine have become interlocking concepts. In a subtle way, so have "marriage" and "colleagueship." When they participate in panels, workshops, or symposia, combining their foci on education and nursing, they tie their minds together. When they share the other parts of family life, they tie together their emotions and memories. The more ties a couple have, the more closely they are bonded. Before long, some of the old dicta about friendship begin to make a weightier sense. "The other half of my soul" is no longer just poetry; "my friend is another self" becomes a richer and richer saying. For, as a matter of fact, the one who complements my inmost spirit, mentally as well as emotionally, *is* my *amicus amicorum*, the most special of my acquaintances. The one who can fill in for me at work as well as in the kitchen *is* an equal through and through.

With proper changes, we can say the same things about the friends to whom we are not married. Whatever the bond between us—recreation, work, or simply affection—it is a tie that makes us more ourselves, a commitment that increases our freedom. Again and again, the love of friendship, like the love of God, works this strange paradox. "O God, to serve whom is to reign," the ancient collect put it. "O friend, to share with whom is to increase my wealth," we might extend the parallel. A brother joined to a brother is like a strong city, the Bible teaches each generation. David's friendship for Jonathan was one of his most winning traits. Practically and emotionally, theologically and in commonplace terms, the love of friendship keeps the world more shining than dulled, more welcoming than rejecting. So if you find a good friend, cling to him or her as to precious rubies. When you meet a sympathetic mind, take a memo to keep in touch. At the grass-roots, the future church seems to be budding forth in many small cells of friendship. If so, it has a good evangelical charter: "I have not called you servants but friends" (Jn 15:15).

Colleagueship

Once I worked in a university department that prided itself on its colleagueship. "The great thing about this department," I was told shortly after arriving, "is the way people connect with one another, the wonderful colleagueship." As I waited for this great gift to bestow itself, I wondered what form it would take. Would people work together developing new courses? Would they conceive joint writing projects? Maybe their main sharing would be purely intellectual, a stimulating exchange of views. Or maybe people would just pair off according to their natural interests, trusting one another enough to set forth their most exciting ideas like fragile trial balloons.

As it approached the end of the first semester, and colleagueship had yet to knock at my door, I started to prowl the corridors, asked my wife to vouch for my deodorant, and generally reassessed my stock. Finally it all came clear, at the departmental Christmas party. There, once again, I heard the canonical tale of the department's wonderful collegiality, but this time I noticed that it contained nary a specific detail. Reflecting back on the other times I had heard the tale told, I realized that "colleagueship" *never* had a specific referent in this department. *Always* it was a pious hope, a myth grown dear simply by frequent narration. Those people did not want colleagueship. They wanted the *idea* of colleagueship, the pennant flying but no solid ship.

Perhaps matters are different in other fields of work, but somehow I suspect they are not. Certainly I have heard much more talk of wonderful religious community than I have ever seen catalytic sharing. And certainly my eyes start to glaze when I hear company men speak about team spirit. No, my somewhat researched suspicion is that working together in truly significant ways, so that sharing deeply benefits all parties, is one of the rarest species of grass-roots community. People have to communicate too openly, adapt too instinctively, set too much ego aside for colleagueship to occur very often. A lot of talk: certainly, that occurs everywhere. Many superficial influences: no problem; we are all somewhat with whom we commute. But collaboration, genuine partnership in creative work: that is a major accomplishment. Like Simon paired with Garfunkel, it makes a music neither partner can come close to creating alone.

Still, on the border between friendship and colleagueship lie many opportunities for sharing personal aspects of our work, and fumbling these opportunities is a central way we abort both friendship and colleagueship. Once again, the best illustration may be the most concrete.

In another university department, far from the scene of the first crimes, I once welcomed a bright-eyed newcomer (having myself now advanced to senior status). Our fields were not similar, nor our personal priorities, but he was good fun, witty and warm-hearted. So, when he professed keen interest in several books I had written, I gave him autographed copies. "I can hardly wait to get to them," he said, and we agreed that we'd soon have a good discussion. After several months with no response, I ventured to tease him and test the waters. Many apologies, a little blushing, and more agreement to meet soon for an engrossing discussion. Of course my expectations were low, but I was intrigued with the funny rituals. The man clearly didn't want to exert himself, yet he couldn't not bow to the prevailing myth. Now, years later, my writing is high on our index of forbidden conversations. Reading a "friend's" book proved too great a task for this man whose daily work is reading. Neither simple curiosity nor plighted troth could move the wheels to turn. Thus does our collegiality go aglimmering.

The first requisite for collegiality, as for so many other human relations, is simple courtesy. If two people extend one another the courtesy of doing what they say they will do, standing by their word, they have a chance to collaborate. If they cannot bring themselves to do what they say they will do (when they say they will do it), they only end up thinking less of human nature.

One can see this positively in circles of friends who work well together. Say that it is a matter of a liturgy group, where the established rule is that the meeting shifts from house to house biweekly. If all honor this rule, informing others when they cannot make the meeting, or when they are unable to host it, the group will move along smoothly, growing in confidence that all know what is happening and all actively support it. Another example might be a partnership in construction, where one person takes charge of outside matters (foundation work, framing, and the like) and the other person takes charge of the inside work (trim, painting, and so forth). If each does his share, and keeps the other informed of both his progress and his problems, the partnership has a fine chance of thriving. If either partner doesn't communicate well, or doesn't fulfill the pledges he or she makes, the partnership is headed for hard times.

Everywhere, then, collaborative work depends upon courtesy and fulfilling one's word. Everywhere we either keep building stronger ties, increasing our trust in one another, or we find that our ties are fraying. From the perspective of Christian faith, our ties at work are a form of neighborly love. From the perspective of Christian faith, colleagueship is a central way we can fulfill Jesus' second great command.

The Local Church[2]

The grass-roots community of most interest to theologians lately has been the local church. Inspired by experiments in Latin America and Europe, many American theologians and pastors have begun to rethink the prospects for smaller church cells.[3] If the Latin American model were to hold, such cells would be quite political. Pressured by their threatening circumstances, many Christians in such countries as Brazil, Chile, Argentina, and El Salvador have banded together to pray, discuss, and forge ways to try to move their countries toward justice. For them the Scriptures have become revolutionary documents, lenses setting local conditions vividly aglow. Jesus' simple bearing and loving program contrast so dramatically with the tyrannies to which they are being subjected that following Jesus seems to entail a wholehearted resistance to the prevailing powers. Individual Christians in these groups may debate particular tactics. They completely agree that Jesus must set their agenda, and that Jesus demands a praxis of justice. If the person who says he loves God and hates his brother is categorically a liar, how much worse is the person who brutalizes his brothers and sisters, keeping them in abject poverty and murdering them if they so much as cry out in protest?

The European grass-roots churches also tend to have a political orientation. For them the arms race, social justice, or ecological goals tend to be the rallying points. In each case, the Gospel and the political goal in question interact dialectically. The views of Jesus provide a ground-level critique of current inhumanities, while current inhumanities sharpen the Gospel to a keen cutting edge. As with the Christians of the Latin American *comunidades de base*, the Europeans' dialectic gives their faith a new energy. Where "culture Christianity" has grown wan and boring, a new prophetic religion, focused on human liberation, brings many to a great awakening: the Spirit seems manifestly to list in the winds of change that have begun stirring. On the horizon gleam wonderful new social arrangements that easily could come into being, were people to put off their old sloth and self-serving. The great need, then, is conversion.

For small groups of Christians in the United States these political orientations can seem equally alluring. Certainly we play a major role in the injustices that now pit the whole earth, especially the injustices of Latin America, and certainly the arms race, economic imbalances, sexual oppressions, racial inequities, and ecological crises crowd any informed agenda at home. Lately, however, I have been thinking about the practical problems of creating grass-roots *ecclesiolae*, local "little churches" that body forth the one catholic whole, and my thoughts have run up against the American way of money. Perhaps meditating on this way will clarify how radical an ecclesiology the future may require of us.

While I am aware that the thrust toward communal owner-ship is a staple in utopian movements, and that most of these movements peter out before they have achieved anything more than a symbolic witness,[4] I yet find myself discovering again and again that the line between acquaintances and friends or broth-ers and sisters in Christ runs along the border of our financial possessions and worries. We don't dare to get close enough to one another to become a familial body, because that would require starting to take responsibility for one another's practical needs. Indeed, it would mean owning up to the ways that our relations, even in good church gatherings, mirror the socio-eco-nomic disparities of the surrounding culture at large. For exam-ple, if one family is able to build a fine new house, while another feels financially bound to rent, they have a lot of distance to cover, on the way to becoming members of one another in any full-bodied sense. Accepting the prevailing American mores, they probably choose not to open the cans of finance, thinking them full of worms. Experience has shown them, or their parents who started inculcating prudential economics as soon as they were high enough to hear whispers have told them, that money matters are best kept secret. So our culture thinks it shameful (even in circles led by the poor Christ) not to be making a fat salary, and shameful to be doing well (because bound to be tainted by lucre). The tacit ideal is the pious millionaire, rolling in riches but humble, generous, and refined. Never mind how hard it is to gain millions without profiting from an unjust finan-cial system. The elect of the new Israel float above the laws of supply and demand; riches prove their divine applehood.

Therefore, to get an American grass-roots ecclesiology going, we would have to struggle with the most knotty of faith's problems: determining what is reasonable to expect of human nature. Does the detritus of the previous communal movements prove that sharing financial resources, becoming members of one another in the most practical ways, is simply beyond most peo-ple's capacities? How does the mixed testimony of the religious orders (communally poor in theory, usually something less than poor or communal in fact) factor in? Is the present need perhaps for beginning gestures, modest movements toward greater openness, real sharing of one another's cares? The old and the young might make the most natural partners, since their financial securities and energies can vary in inverse proportions. If old people who were even modestly secure financially were to take a practical interest in the financial struggles of energetic young people, and young people were to take a practical interest in the worries of the old, we might see green sprouts of fresh church life springing up in all sorts of unlikely places.

Liturgy

The family, friendship, colleagueship, and the local church all point to potential grass-roots communities, fledgling cells of the body catholic. Is there a privileged way to focus God's love upon these communities, a new angle that might get us around the barriers that prevent their full construction? In my experience, one of the best ways has been the liturgy, eucharistic Christian worship. When the Spirit of prayer gathers two or three in Christ's name, and the millennial symbols of bread and wine swell to pregnancy, the group members can be hushed to catch overtones they usually miss, hallowed so that grace becomes perceptible. None of this happens automatically. Our climate of rush and chatter makes liturgy a demanding work. But happen liturgy does, for the Spirit is not constrained.

The liturgy tells a story since, as Elie Wiesel has reminded us, "God made man because he loves stories." The "he" in that sentence is ambiguous, one suspects deliberately so. Wiesel is saying that human beings love stories, come to attention when they hear "once upon a time." He is also saying that God seems to love stories, to have stayed true to his description of himself in Exodus: I am as I shall be with you. So, God is for us as our history of living with God, probing the divine Mystery, being defeated by the impenetrability of Beginning and Beyond, shows divinity to be.[5] It is not the abstractions that teachers chalk upon the board that best point to God's "nature." It is the experience God's people have had trying to hold hands with a Holy Spirit, doing their best to grow more and more human, as the dictates of their consciences have prodded them.

Specifically, the Christian eucharistic liturgy tells the story of Jesus' passover from life to death to life again. After pausing to open their hearts and arrest their minds, Christians gathered for the liturgy plunge back into this biblical story. They want to refresh their sense of what happened "back then," when the blueprint of their worldview was sketched, but they want even more to contact again the ongoing tale of their people, the family saga determining their names. According to the pericopes and symbols of their official ceremonies, they should be the people who have gone down with Jesus in the hope of rising with Jesus, the people that once sat in darkness and now has seen a great light. The rub, and so much of the "problem" with today's Christian liturgy, is the rarity of such an identification. Only in the most unusual circumstances does a group gathered to express its unity in Christ's name define itself this way the other days of the month. By and large, most of us do our business, take our recreation, ponder "the way things are" with but passing reference to the living mystery of Jesus, the present power of the Spirit.

The reason is not our moral turpitude. The reason is our neutral or irreligious atmosphere. The information that floods our senses day and night takes little of its form from Jesus. Newscasters, bosses, and peers put huge brackets around Jesus, either because they scarcely think of God's man, or because they are afraid of sounding fundamentalist. One can sympathize with this fear, yet think there might be an alternative. Were we able to refer to God the Father, Jesus, and the Spirit as somewhat empirical entities, the Mystery as real and significant as the air we breathe and the headlines we read, our speech could be both religious and straightforward. Then death, suffering, struggle, doubt, and all the other incursions of our finitude and sinfulness would not be omitted from our general discourse (with a hundred bad effects). Then life, joy, grace, conviction, and all the other touches of divinity and possibility could be operative thoughts in our brains (with a hundred good effects).

The liturgy can work this linguistic and conceptual transformation, because it can make the world of religion real. At least to myself, in those capital moments of quiet matins or late compline, I can say with complete honesty something like:

> Sunday night, after the discussion, when Jill and Bob had settled their differences and we moved to the Offertory, I did, incontrovertibly, feel a special peace, a surge of joy, that convinced me of the Spirit. Self-evidently, with no need for further reference, it was good to be there, good to be being changed. Once again, I felt the Mystery of being alive. Once again, everything was loosened up. The dead-ends seemed to swing open. A dozen new beginnings swam into view. "Behold, I make all things new," the Christ of Revelation whispered. "It is only necessary to stand at the door and knock." Nothing need separate us from the love of God in Christ Jesus. No old failures need control God's tomorrow.

Live liturgy sings of these things, is imaginative and alert like the Book of Revelation. Granted its bloodthirstiness and dangers of imbalance, Revelation is still an irreplaceable Christian poetry. How else would we know how to describe his voice like the sound of rushing waters? Who else has drawn hair white as wool, eyes like a flame of fire, feet like burnished bronze, a face like the sun shining in full strength? When we love such liturgical images, we blast away the torpor and fatigue that usually depress our spirits. With such burdens removed, our spirits can begin the love of community, the creativity that makes others significant. "The Church" should name our most significant others, be the place where the people who round our edges and feed our health come into their wholest pattern.

Chapter Six
Diet and Health

Sane Eating

There are four primal zones to reality: nature, society, the self, and divinity. In Chapter Two, dealing with ecology, we considered nature's place in the whole that we are trying to fill with God's love. Chapters Three, Four, and Five dealt with society, under the headings of economics, politics, and grass-roots communities. Now we turn to the self. Chapters Six through Ten will explore different aspects of our personal lives, under the conviction that we ourselves must be the main agents of the changes necessary to make a holistic life-style take hold. In Chapter Eleven we will bend back to our beginning, returning to the theological concerns we sketched in Chapter One. The overall pattern of the book, therefore, is a mandala, a symbol of wholeness. As he must be in any work truly Christian, God is the alpha and the omega, gathering together all the parts of creation that nature, society, and our selves represent.

Our chapters on the self deal with what many readers probably expected "holistic spirituality" to connote. In the past "spirituality" has been conceived as rather personal, if not individualistic, so matters such as health, play, sex, education, and meditation have played determining (if sometimes tacit) roles. I have deliberately begun this holistic spirituality with ecological and social issues, to make the point that today holism cannot pit the individual against the environment or the group. Holism is an option for both/and rather than either/or. Both the environment and the individual are key ingredients in God's creation. Both society and the self must be coordinated if we are to have gracious political and personal lives. Therefore, in turning to the more explicitly personal issues we are not entering the domain of "spirituality" for the first time. All that went before is as candidate for God's love as what is now to follow.

As though to press home this point, the topic of diet and health rubs our noses in the relations between ourselves and the surrounding environment.[1] Through our bodies we are spirits-in-the-world, personalities significantly shaped by what we eat. That is one of the main motivations and findings of the new concern for a sane diet. Although we in the modern West have extended human longevity, largely by conquering infectious diseases through improved sanitation, antibiotics, and immunization programs, we are dying from chronic, diet-related diseases at rates dramatically higher than those of even our recent forebears.

After infancy, human beings have no natural instinct for what food is wholesome and what unnourishing. To have a healthy diet, we must study and choose. Studying, we find that many peoples of the world do not have the concentrations of meats and fats in their diets that we Americans recently have developed. Their diets, which have stayed more traditional, are high in starches and vegetable sources of protein, low in meats, fats, and sugars. As long as they maintain their traditional diets they do not have the chronic health problems we do, the clogged arteries and afflicted bowels, but when they switch to our type of diet, these problems soon develop. Japan is a case in point. As post-war affluence has caused Japanese to increase their intake of meat significantly, the incidence of heart disease in Japan has risen significantly.

Even in terms of recent American history, our dietary patterns have shifted for the worse. Since 1910, when the United States Department of Agriculture began keeping records of the American diet, the amounts of meat, fish, poultry, alcohol, soft drinks, and sugar that we eat have risen dramatically. By contrast, our consumption of milk, grain products, fresh fruit, and vegetables has declined equally dramatically. Where we now obtain about 70 percent of our protein from animal sources rich in fat and cholesterol, at the turn of the century 50 percent of our protein came from grains, beans, and similar sources low in fat and virtually free of cholesterol.[2] Today 60 percent of our calories come from fats or added sugars. Fat consumption went up 31 percent from 1910 to 1976, while starch consumption declined 43 percent. From 1910–1976 per capita beef consumption increased 72 percent, chicken consumption 179 percent, cheese consumption 388 percent, processed fruit consumption 500 percent, margarine consumption 681 percent, and the consumption of ice cream products 1426 percent.[3] Total calorie consumption per capita has declined about 3 percent since 1910, but our lifestyle is so much more sedentary that this decline is far too little.

So, we are eating our way to bad health. When one combines the more dangerous diet we have adopted with the higher stress of our current life-styles, the result is an insane, highly injurious pattern of eating. The stewardship we have for our bodies, the care that any loving Creator would expect, has gone out the window, multiplying our medical problems and decreasing our ability to perform. The quality of the life closest to us, the life of our personal body-mind composite, surely has declined, causing us to feel the world, inhabit our flesh and exercise our potential with much less return to God, much less interest on the Creator's investment than we ought to have been paying. If the parable of the talents (Mt 25:14–30) tells us something perennial about God's expectations, our diets are bringing us into deep religious trouble. We are not only hurting ourselves. We are abusing God's generosity, denying that we do not belong to ourselves.

On the positive front, proposals from such impressive sources as Senator George McGovern's 1977 Select Committee on Nutrition and Human Needs have established new nutritional guidelines that could turn our eating habits around. The Committee predicted an 80 percent drop in the number of obese Americans, a 25 percent drop in deaths from heart disease, a 50 percent drop in deaths from diabetes, and a 1 percent annual

increase in longevity if Americans would eat less fat, less cholesterol, less refined and processed sugars, less salt, less alcohol, less
calories, and more complex carbohydrates and roughage. Overall, the Committee's target was a new diet that would be about
30 percent fats, 12 percent proteins, and 58 percent carbohydrates. Compared to the typical American diet of the mid-1970's,
this meant decreasing fat intake about 12 percent and increasing
carbohydrate intake about 12 percent. The good news is that,
through a growing movement for better nutrition, millions of
people have gotten behind proposals like the Committee's,
including the Departments of Agriculture and Health, Education, and Welfare.

Wellness

As the facts about diet, nutrition, stress, and other aspects of
our current American life-style have begun to roll in, many
professionals (and amateurs) have come to see the need for a
turnaround. Because hitherto most of our thinking about health
has been negative, focused on how to repair injuries or cure disease, an entire positive dimension has remained relatively unex-
ploited. Calling this positive dimension *wellness*, these professionals have started to describe ways by which we might
enhance the quality of our lives, making health not just the
absence of disease but the presence of a high-level energy and
sense of well-being.

In one of Donald Ardell's best-selling books on wellness,
five dimensions stand forth.[4] The central, core dimension is what
he calls "self-responsibility." In the inventory that Ardell offers
for rating one's current self-responsibility, the first statement is
the tip-off: "My health is affected more by what I do or do not
do than it is by doctors, circumstances, fate, the gods, drugs, hospitals, and other factors out of my control." Three choices confront the reader: yes, I agree; no, I disagree; not sure. The self-
responsible person obviously checks "yes, I agree." Wellness
begins with personal responsibility, realizing that how one feels
is largely a function of one's own choices.

Thus the people at the lowest levels of Ardell's scale have chosen (either actively or passively) to lack exercise, abuse alcohol, rely on nicotine or caffeine, be obese, casually use tranquilizers, have unrealistic expectations regarding the medical system, and esteem themselves very little. Wellness progresses by making choices, managing changes, that move one away from these bad options.

A second dimension of wellness is nutritional awareness. This has several component parts. How did my parents teach me to regard food—as a matter of reward or punishment? Do I now use food as an entertainment? Do I regularly consume processed meat, colas, sugar-loaded cereals, or fast foods? Do I know that exercise usually depresses the appetite and so aids weight control? The point to such questions is to bring eating out of the dark forest of irrationality and into the open plain of intelligent choice. To gobble down food while one is excited, paying little heed to what one is eating or how it has been prepared, is to open a Pandora's box of digestive, weight, and nutritional troubles. To learn something about the nutritional values of different foods or methods of preparation, and make dining a leisurely, aesthetically pleasing experience, is to open a treasure trove of wellness.

A third dimension in Ardell's scheme of wellness is physical fitness. Helpful in this regard is an inventory of one's attitudes toward physical activity. Am I more a participant or a spectator? Is there a physical activity that I regularly enjoy? Does this activity help endurance, strength, and flexibility? Do I feel good about the way my body looks? If my answers to questions such as these are affirmative, I am probably providing for my physical fitness quite well. If they are negative, I probably have yet to appreciate the importance of exercise. In that case, I probably also underestimate aerobic conditioning, heart recovery rate, ratio of body fat to lean muscle, and other indices of my physical base for wellness. Quite likely I don't think of my body as a rich potential put into my hands and am far from happy with the way I look in the mirror.

Stress is a fourth dimension of wellness. To deal with it, such techniques as bio-feedback, deep breathing, centering and balancing exercises have emerged. Among the signs of high levels of stress, or poor stress management, are sleeping badly, twitching, having cold hands and feet, feeling aches in the neck or shoulders, and taking setbacks badly. Such signs suggest that one is tight, lacks the proper give, has constricted the range of emotions that ideally one would possess. The result is a diminished receptivity to experience, and a diminished reaction as well. The body suffers more wear and tear than it should, at times to the point of danger. Wellness therefore includes the ability to handle the stresses that inevitably occur in one's life, and to avoid the stresses that are unnecessary. The better one's management of stress, the more enjoyable and efficient one's functioning.

A fifth dimension of wellness is what Ardell calls sensitivity to one's environment. For example, am I alert to the ways that poor health habits have been made to seem normal: ashtrays on restaurant tables, alcohol standard at parties? How often do I enjoy a belly laugh? Is my self-image positive, my store of self-destructive impulses low? Do my friends have positive outlooks, attitudes that enhance wellness all around? What level of possessions do I desire, and what impact do I make upon the general fund of natural resources? The point is the *climate* in which I live and move, my ideas, associates, and sense of nature. To achieve high level wellness, one needs an environment that is supportive, does not assault one's health.

So, although the key to wellness is personal responsibility, nutrition, physical fitness, stress, and one's environment also play important parts. We can move toward good health, a sense of well-being, if we are willing to bring diet, exercise, relaxation, and positive thinking to our aid. "Well-being is less mystical than we have been led to believe, more empirical and practical," the gurus of the wellness movement proclaim. If grace perfects nature, the theologian can second most wellness programs enthusiastically.

Holistic Medicine

When modern science turned health care in an empirical direction, and then enabled dramatic advancements in the cure of infectious diseases and the development of new techniques of intervention, medicine turned to paradigms of specialization. In the past twenty years, however, these paradigms have come in for serious reconsideration, since it has become clear that specialized medicine is not doing an adequate job. For example, as of 1974 fifty percent of American deaths came from cardiovascular and cerebrovascular disease, and another nineteen percent came from cancer. Other recent figures are similarly alarming: "Twenty-four million Americans currently have hypertension (a major predisposing cause of both cardiovascular and cerebrovascular disease), and a like number are afflicted with sleep-onset insomnia. Twice as many have regular headaches and three times the number are more than twenty pounds above their optimal weight. A recent report by the President's Commission on Mental Health (1978) tells us that 9 million Americans are alcoholic and that '15 percent of our population needs some form of mental health services.'"[5]

Figures such as these, and the suffering individuals they represent, have caused a reappraisal of the American health care system, and this reappraisal in turn has involved a number of significant sub-critiques. For instance, our high use of surgery and drugs has come in for criticism, as well as our neglect of emotional factors. Research techniques borrowed from family therapy, sociology, and anthropology suggest that emotional illnesses are closely tied to a patient's economic and social situation, while relativity theory has opened room for physicians to admit the subjective factor in their diagnoses. The light shed by spiritual regimes, both new and traditional, has encouraged some physicians to allow for religious factors, and the new political awareness fostered by the war in Vietnam has put the demographic data on disease (who gets what kinds of diseases and what kinds of treatment) in the spotlight, along with the capitalistic aspects of the lucrative medical industry. From ecologists have come studies linking air pollution, urban overcrowding, and toxic chemicals with high incidences of disease. From consumer advocates has come a cry for less expensive, more effective, and more humane health care systems, rooted in local communities. Humanists have argued for a medical practice that deals with feelings and interpersonal relations better than the specialist model. People aware of how other cultures practice medicine have argued for opening American medicine to the wisdoms of other traditions. Meanwhile, the economic crisis of American health care has escalated. With the expenses of our national health care rising toward two hundred billion dollars annually (and rising at twice the rate of other sectors of the economy), finding a better way has become a matter of strict financial exigency.

The result has been the evolution, at least in some parts of the health care community, of a new paradigm, called holistic medicine. Among its characteristics are: trying to care for the physical, mental, and spiritual aspirations of its patients (looking upon them as wholes); trying to treat people as individuals, with unique genetic, biological, and psychosocial endowments; trying to take into account a patient's particular culture, family context, and local community; looking upon health as a positive state, rather than as the absence of disease; emphasizing the promotion of health and the prevention of disease; stressing people's personal responsibility for their health; trying to help patients mobilize their capacities for healing themselves, without denying the need on occasion for dramatic interventions such as surgery; stressing education and self-care; being open to a variety of diagnostic methods and interpretational systems; encouraging physical, "hands on" contact between physicians and patients; emphasizing good nutrition and vigorous exercise; appreciating the positive place of sensuousness and sexuality; trying to make illness an opportunity for discovery; trying to raise the quality of each phase of a person's life; appreciating the setting in which health or disease is occurring, and so encouraging intimate home or hospice sites for care; trying to understand and change the socio-economic conditions that perpetuate ill health; and changing the views of medical practitioners away from the prevailing narrowness.[7]

In this encouraging list of characteristics one sees a kinship between holistic medicine and the holistic Christian spirituality we have been developing. Both stress taking into account the full range of data or influences and being sensitive to the interconnectedness of the human being's many different aspects. True, where holistic medicine stresses the person's wellness, a Christian spirituality stresses the centrality of God's gracious love. But these two stresses are not inimical. Indeed, a generous theology of grace suspects that the inspiration of humane movements such as holistic medicine finally comes from the Spirit, while a liberal holistic medicine does not rule out the ultimacy of divine mystery. Of course, where Christian theology ponders such metaphysical problems as evil and creativity, holistic medicine is more comfortable with tests and conferences. But each study offers the other a balance or complement. Thus Donald Ardell's six "life areas" (optimal health, business/profession, money/financial security, self-development, having fun, primary relationships/family)[6] might receive considerable deepening from the historical or ontological horizons of the great religions, while a holistic program such as Ardell's could be just the shot in the arm many depressed church people desperately need.

Aging

The continuum along which all our bodily concerns must move is the process of our aging. From a religious perspective this continuum is a blessing, because it pressures us to deal with the ultimate pattern of things and wears away our narcissism. We are all sufficiently interested in ourselves (note that Jesus could assume this interest: "Love your neighbor as yourself") to run the risk of self-absorption. The dynamics of work and parenthood push against our self-absorption, as do the dynamics of healthy worship, but the continuum of aging is the most inevitable prod.

As death grows closer and closer, the need to make sense of one's whole time and whole environment usually grows apace. Thus people become interested in history, which seems to offer a story they might make their own. They delve into philosophy, which tries to map the heavens. Philanthropy beckons to many as a way to leave a permanent mark. Health also becomes a dominant interest, as aches increase and years become more precious.

To age with energy and grace, a simplified and healthy regime is almost requisite. If we abuse our bodies year after year, we will find them unable to provide us the second half of life we would like. To help us construct simple, practicable regimes that might maximize our enjoyment of the second half of life, holistic physicians and nurses have focused on some elementary habits. Walking, for example, does wonders for the overall tone of the body, and running even more. Not only does good exercise pump the blood and fill the lungs, it trims the waist and tightens the teeth. Deep breathing is another simple habit, practical for almost all. When we breathe shallowly, we not only limit our supply of oxygen, we also fail to exercise our spongy inner organs. As simple a habit as breathing deeply four times a day for six seconds relaxes the body and aids many of its organs.

There are similarly simple dietary habits that can help our bodies age well. For example many chronically ill people drink very little water. Yet drinking good amounts of water each day is a main way to flush the system and remove impurities. Relatedly, fiber has come into our national consciousness lately, in good part because of our many digestive problems. Research studies seem to show that when a diet is generous in fruits, vegetables, and grains, problems of the lower bowel practically disappear. And so the advocates of simplified living can continue to offer easy counsels: people who stay away from large doses of animal fats have few problems of heart disease; women who avoid fats have a low incidence of ovarian and breast cancers; people who meditate or "center down" have fewer digestive problems.

Many of these observations confirm age-old common sense. Too much haste and pressure cause an acid stomach. Regular, balanced meals smooth the way to long years of feeling good. The sweat of good exercise seems to get the poisons out. Sufficient sleep and relaxation help the whole person to unwind. The folk wisdom of most peoples is full of dicta such as these. If the goal is to live one's time well, to age in a way that is ripening, a simple regime of sound diet and strong exercise is a capital way to succeed.

We also have to come to grips with aging psychologically. Even if our bodies stay in good health, our minds continue to change. We take on different relations to the generations behind us and before as we ourselves grow older. Usually, we gain more responsibility at work, more status in our local communities. Everywhere, the expectation is that we will manifest an increasing maturity, wisdom, and accomplishment. Insofar as we do not meet this expectation (and few of us ever fully can), we have to come to grips with who it seems we have become. At twenty we may become any one of several people. By forty-five, who we are has largely arrived.

I do not mean, of course, that we cannot grow through our fifties, sixties, and seventies. Any day given to us is an opportunity for growth. But the later growth tends to be subtler, a matter of appropriating, consolidating, and extending collateral lines. With the main foundation laid, there is time and need for embellishment, extension, appreciation. Having gotten up a good head of steam, one can get into easy striding. The blessing of easy striding, mainly maintaining good momentum, is a chance to enjoy the journey more. Getting up to pace is hard work, all-absorbing and highly stressful. Maintaining momentum is less demanding, leaving one freer to consider the lilies of the field, how they grow, the children of one's children, how they charm. It allows time for culture, if one is willing to lend an ear. It affords a better appreciation of food, clothing, and other staples. Politics invites those who are mature and still have good digestion, for the systemic quality of most of our evils grows clear by middle age. Good example invites any with compassion, for truth and love seem everywhere to be in far too short supply. Finally, everywhere there is traditioning: handing on what has been received. For faith this is the most important obligation: to keep the darkness at bay.

"Vanity of vanities and all is vanity," the weary wise man exclaimed. The passing of time shows us to indulge many foolishnesses. But if we can get into patterns that secure us physical and mental health, much less will seem vain and foolish. "For every thing there is a season, and for every time a purpose under heaven." That was the wise man on a good day, a stretch when all seemed well.

Chapter Seven
Exercise and Play

Exercise

Our central thesis is that wholeness comes from letting the love of God flow out from the center of our selves to the different zones we are invited to indwell. A second personal zone that the self may indwell is exercise and play. In exercise we work the body for the sake of toning it, bringing it to peak performance. In play we work the body-mind composite for the sake of freeing it, opening it to new sources of energy and encouragement. Neither sort of "work" should be oppressive. Both should be enjoyable, a matter of doing something we have been made to do.

We have been made to exercise. A priori this flows from our being animals, related to lions, tigers, and baboons. If we lack their speed, grace, and strength, we share their need to flex the muscles and work off the calories that dominate our physical systems. Out of shape is out of kilter, out of line. Often it is depressing and stressful, out of sorts. Nothing clears the spleen like an hour's hard running. With something to burn, the body can cut loose, give the spirit a much needed break. Most of us run into three or four difficult problems every week. Solving them can raise large quantities of tension, and sometimes even anger. But tension and anger are perfect fuels for exercise. Run those laps, hit that tennis ball, bash that punching bag—as though you were stomping your problems to bits. Soon you will be able to smile calmly through many trying times, knowing that exercise and relief are just around the corner.

Paul spoke about the bodily vessel we carry, how its mortality makes it ill-fit our spirits, how its closeness to divine life should govern its use. If only the tubby vessels floating in my harbor would take themselves to the training pool. In three months they could be sleek and happy. Granted, the oxygen highs and chemical improvements that exercise brings are not the stuff of nirvana. George Sheehan and the other running gurus who overplay the animality theme have sold much of their faith for thirty pieces of paganism. But psychologists have discovered that hard exercise helps many who suffer depression, and dozens of exercise salons shout that firm muscle tone is now both fashion and glamor. Feeling good and looking good can brighten not a few dark days. For Christians schooled in the sacraments, they can give God another set of icons.

The value of exercise that I would stress, however, is its lessons in humanity. A cerebral, computerized time merely complicates a now centuries-old problem: How do we put mind and body back together again? Some commentators make Plato the source of this problem, others blame Descartes, but all of us wrestle with its tensions. Unless we use our bodies well, we ignore a major part of our identity. Unless we get ourselves into good shape, we never know how the world might look, sound, smell, taste, and feel. Ideally, we all would study ballet, which combines hard muscular work with grace and music. Ideally, we would all grow up knowing in our capillaries why T. S. Eliot saw human time as a dance.

The dancer or well-trained actress knows things through, with, and in her body that pass the rest of us by. What for us is murky in perception or expression is for her clear and self-possessed. So she is the more lucid and enriched, we the muddier and poorer. For she has exercised her embodied self, while we have lounged and loafed. Our range of humanity is constricted. The potential God gave us is unplumbed. Once again those biblical talents become our accusers. How could we not know we were supposed to become lithe and well-conditioned? What master craftsman could make such a marvel as the human body and not be disappointed when we allow it to rust? Still, I would have the tone of these questions be more sorrow than outrage. These days outrage is too much with us, and too little profitable. Those ever earnest soon are ever tiresome, like rain falling on a tin roof. It is the edge of sadness that I would pry, the regret at another praise and joy being lost.

Under a blue sky, feeling a stiff breeze, the Kansas veteran begins his workout with an act of faith. He doesn't feel like lighting the fires and oiling the gears, but past experience tells him it is good he should. The cold that nips him will soon be merely bracing. The joints so stiff will soon unfold. So he starts his plod, feeling a little foolish when the supple coeds flash by. The first half of his workout is dull work, twenty minutes or so of mild penance. With the second wind, however, recompense starts coming in. Soon it is good measure, packed down and overflowing. His sweatsuit is off, his legs are bare, and he wants to pour it on. For three glorious laps he is perfect, a Walter Mitty Olympian. Way back in his gene pool, once upon a distant time, his ancestors ran like this most of the day, thirty or forty miles.

The veteran has found other things to occupy his time, some of them much loftier, but what his ancestors did was far from wrong or ignoble. They used what God had given them, ran with spirits open to the heavens. So, every once in a while, he runs for the sheer heaven of it, the sheer rightness of using a divine gift. Then, ending sweaty and out of breath, he gasps a little prayer: "I hope that makes me live a little longer, and I thank you for how good I feel."

Sports

If exercise were to dominate our schools' approach to the body, we would be preparing a healthier generation. Despite progress in this direction, sports often block the way. As long as the paradigm remains hulking football players, physical education will remain a poor relation. At my school, where the NCAA stops by regularly to penalize, athletics are part of the educational problem. A cottage industry of coaches, players, and administrators caters to a local lust for action. In imitation, kids six and seven don shoulder pads and begin long careers of hard hitting. It would be ludicrous, if it did not warp so many personalities.

The advent of women's athletics is helping somewhat, making many spectators take a second look at form and skill, but with both men and women now swearing by weights or praying to the god of mental toughness, sports are losing their savor. The good aspect of competition, its calling forth our best, is ceding to the Nietzschean aspect, the diabolical will to power. Add in the enormous monies we pay top professionals and you have a very dubious entertainment. In their different ways, boxing, football, and car racing have become beautiful forms of mayhem. You cannot serve God and mayhem.

A holistic spirituality, on the lookout for what is good for the body-soul composite, would test each sport critically. When it came across items like artificial turf and rock-hard helmets which practically guarantee a high quota of injuries, it would point the finger of accusation: "For the sake of money and spectator lust, we are scraping limbs and breaking bones. In a strange new perversion of the sabbath, we give hours without end to cracking vertebrae and fracturing knees. Boxing has become little more than Roman games, gore for the worst of the masses. Hockey's goons, trained like Dobermans, exist only to produce violence. Away with them. They've lost their license to amuse."

The recreations we employ, like the foods we eat, should be in the service of our nourishment. As it is a major scandal that so much food in our supermarkets is full of noxious sugars, salts, and preservatives, so it is a major scandal that violent amusements dominate so much education and popular culture. Because of the money in it, the public sloth, the paleolithic lack of imagination, a giant distraction industry now holds millions of our people in thrall. In the future, we may compound this with video games, scarcely a more desirable narcotic. Already nature goes unobserved, poor people starve, while millions offer up quarters to Pac-Man. A very strange culture, the late twentieth-century. A weird sort of soul-loss.

That is probably the crux: Does a sport, a game, help us to gain or lose our souls? In healthy sport, the play is the thing. Entering a new, artificial world, one stands free of customary inhibitions, can try a few tricks for their own sake, as ends in themselves. So on a glorious morning, while others sleep, one drives a little ball down a fairway. To hit the ball high and straight has no more meaning than the arc of one's swing, its pleasure to the touch and the eye. Golf is a foolish game and a lovely game, a wealth of useful distraction. Taken for this, kept at this, it is another song to human ingenuity. Worked over and over, lavished with care, it becomes more than a little foolish. The Japanese sects that have turned golf into Shinto, using it to pay homage to the *kami*, show the final logic of athletic addiction. Contrariwise, the zen of golf is a forgetting of self, so that reality may be transparent. If Christianity is true, the most transparent reality is the Spirit of God, who never lets us become too distracted.

Is God then not sportive? By no means. The Wisdom of God played before him, when the world was taking form. Sport, in the sense of free play, imaginative worlds, tells us a great deal about the divine nature. But all in order, proportion, good balance. When the world has distributive justice, let a thousand country clubs bloom. When football can replace war, let coaching be our main ministry. The problem in our sports is their imbalance, their refusal to stay in their place. Like many of our creations, they keep tending toward idolatry. Muslims say that idolatry is the cardinal sin, the source of all other disorders.

Aesthetics

Aesthetics deal with the beautiful, one species of which can be athletic grace. When a game is beautifully conceived and beautifully played, it deserves our spirited applause. We can love it enthusiastically, because it has shone with something of God. It has been sacramental, as all creation should be. A holistic spirituality is always trying to see things sacramentally, for the good they would show and be. Always, it is trying to find a handle, gain an edge, that reveals the largess of our Creator. Ugliness and evil are all around—no straight shooter can deny it. But beauty and goodness have more abounded, if the Christian tale is true. Even Pac-Man, that seductive devil, has charms on a given day. Were I not leery of his addling my children's brains, I would delight in his omnivorous little being.

It is better to delight than to decry. It is more whole and fructifying. Among the best helps to delighting are the world's free beauties and humanity's arts. So the Japanese plant cherry trees, to make every spring a benefaction. So even a wretched slum apartment sometimes has a flower box, as a last little resistance of the spirit. In the formative days of my religious upbringing, the place of beauty stood low. We had pleasant surroundings and gorgeous vestments but beauty itself was a seducer. There was the beauty of women, entirely forbidden. There was the beauty of art, almost heretical. For marines of the spirit such as we, beauty seemed soft and peripheral. Yes, the mountains were splendid and ice was grand. Yes, the choir enhanced all the Christmas octave. But our cells were bare, our clothes were stained, and our souls were rather arid. We were young, and so somewhat to be excused, but too many of us have never grown older.

Lately I have begun to age, my beard turning white and grizzly. One of the nicest aspects of this has been the chance to catch up with beauty. Now and then I actually see a flower, wonder at its autumn orange. It wasn't there in May, I dimly recall; someone had to love it in October. And I look at the wood in my house, oiled and finished by a craftsman. It is a roseate oak, with striking grains, and it smells and feels lovely. A blue tile complements this oak, almost cobalt and crystalline. I actually stop thinking, probing, pondering, to take this blue tile in. What might I not make of wife or child, were I to take them in similarly? What might bread and wine not become? Any day there is there, all around me, a passel of sacraments. The fault is not with God's world. The stars do all they should. The fault is with me.

Yes, some of this depends on hormones and clocks—I know that to my humbling. And I shall never see as artists do, since I blunted my senses so long. But all of this is improvable, redeemable, capable of further entry. If I try, I can make some of my

living more gracious. Not in the effete or pretentious way that
caused Kierkegaard to rate the aesthetic type so lowly. In a humble, solid way, like that of an aged Jewish couple I know. They
have done well financially, through medicine and education.
The house they own is lovely without, inside a treasury of art.
But they hold all this lightly, with a striking gratitude. Perhaps
because they are aged, each day's sun or storm seems special.
When they sit at their breakfast table, beside their azure pool,
they give thanks to the Master of the universe for so blessing
them in goods and children. They know some of their wealth is
ill-gotten. They see the systemic wrongs. So they do what they
can through charity, trying to share their good fortune. But they
never deny what they know is true: their world is often beautiful. If Christian immortality were to take away this world, we
should have to rethink its vaunted value.

Jesus, then, must be beautiful. Among all the children of
women, he must have shone with a special glow. Bloodied by
the soldiers, broken on the cross, he yet rose like an Easter lily.
There was no comeliness in him, because of our sin, yet no one
ever spoke like him. So lovely appear, over the mountains, the
feet of them that preach, and bring good news of his peace. So,
like the rainbow, the memory of Jesus should shine forth a
pledge that sordid destruction will never be God's last word. We
especially need this memory these days, as the nuclear menace
mounts. Ugly as sin, our war machines grind away at all our
hopes. The peaceniks, West and East, who put flowers in the
guns of grim soldiers acted better than most of them knew.

The Pope is never going to have many divisions of killers.
The Stalins will never understand. Jesus will go down to the
Herods and Pilates as long as people stay sinners. But Jesus will
rise and speak gently with Marys and Peters, as long as God is
God. How beautiful that Easter story. How fine that their hearts
burned within, flaming up when they came to break the bread.
It is all there, in epitome. Both beauty and sadness are eucharistic. Perhaps that is why the Eucharist is the wholest of our
actions, the one we should best adorn. Simply and elegantly, we
should try to give it whatever perfection we have. If it were our
best time, our best attention, our best sharing, the other days of

the week would be better. If we sang God a simple song, praised God with hearts and flowers, we could endure a great deal more. Beauty is strong, like shoots pushing through a rock. Beauty is supple, like a thousand shades of green bamboo. Beauty is our birthright, if we have eyes to see and ears to hear.

Poetry

If we have imaginations to picture and words to conjure up, we can start to cash in on our birthright. This is what I mean by "poetry": the making *(poesis)* or creative part of our thought and language, the acts reflecting the divine "let there be." Let there be light: openings to more of God's truth. Let there be humor: incongruity, satire, self-depreciation. Let there be love: images to caress the world, bring things to climax, embrace our time in content. In a word, let there be spiritual life: minds and hearts wide awake. Against the torpor of the crowd, their thoughtlessness and crudity, let there be painters and composers, scientists and healers, to uncork the magnums of spirit.

The poetic strikes off the ordinary—the tired, the hackneyed, the dead. When any healthy, fully human soul speaks, the issuance is a poetry. So, sprung from the desert, Jesus waxed parabolic. Out of the fullness of his heart, his mouth spoke ringing words. Oi vey, how Jesus' rhetoric shames us. His tongue would lash, his voice would soothe, and his mind would make wonderful figures. Remember the widow with her mite, how he painted her entry to the temple? Remember the publican and the Pharisee? The one went down to his house justified, while the other only dug his guilt deeper. What sort of a mind must Jesus have had, to have seen and re-formed so well? What brooding over the Scriptures, or listening at his mother's knee, or lonely walks in the dark forged such powerful speaking? The Logos, light of God's light, gave Jesus picture upon picture upon picture. The Spirit, breath of God's love, turned his eye and his heart to compassion. From compassion, he saw and heard and understood—really, as only a parent or lover can. From imagination, he made pictures to carry his compassion: stories, sayings, predictions. If a good heart can warm a good mind, we too can be biblical poets. Indwelling our language, hearing God's word, we too can find a spare eloquence. Yea verily, there was a time when many people spoke well.

At that time, oral tradition bathed all the young in great deeds and noble speech. Be it the Greek aristocrat or the desert Semite, an old set of tales formed each new generation. Out of that formation, the mature person could know himself, see things realistically, and express both knowledge and sight beautifully. When Socrates took this mythic ideal beyond itself to logic, he did not desert the old Greek honor of the beautiful. Similarly, when Jesus brought Israelite prophecy forward, he kept its stirring parallelisms. As the heavens were above the earth, so were Jesus' flights to inspiration. As the word of God did not return to him empty, neither did Jesus' speech. It went forth directly, hit the mark, and returned with a yea or nay. Those struck by Jesus' speech were fixed to a *kairos*, a time of unavoidable decision. Not to choose for Jesus was to choose against Jesus—there were no recesses or lengthy postponements. If today you heard his voice and hardened your heart, God help you on the morrow's judgment.

For those who love to contemplate Jesus, stirring a bit of poetry is not hard. To gain this bit of holism, one need only hush the inner mind. The womb of poetry is silence. The speech of grace comes from quiet. Shut the doors, Lao Tzu said, withdraw within regularly. Then, with no radio, television, or stereo, no noise without or noise within, you can start to explore your iceberg, the seven-eights of you hitherto out of your sight. The world of the spirit is infinitely more fertile and productive than the world of the animal senses. Between the culture of monkeys and the least of our cultures yawns an immeasureable canyon. Poetry is a sort of hang-gliding, a riding of the currents of that canyon up and down. Letting go of terra firma, thinking a fresh new thought, we take off for parts unknown.

Then the Spirit can groan in our spirits, with sighs too deep for words. Then the illuminative way, where Jesus' words beam light, can begin to advance upon us. If we can sing, the light will become good music. If we can bow, the groaning will become a Muslim prayer. Really, though, the modalities are all quite secondary. The first thing is simply to live, begin the life of the spirit. The first thing is what Heraclitus saw: waking up, making an image, thinking a new and personal thought. The beginning of poetry is wakefulness. The end is out of sight. All things end in mystery, the lives of poets most of all.

Chapter Eight
Sexuality

Eros

Much of the love that drives poetry, makes us respond to nature, society, or the self aesthetically, is erotic. We go out to the beautiful desirously as well as appreciatively. We want to touch and possess as well as admire. Partial beings that we are, we long to join ourselves to other beings that might complete us. With both beautiful things and beautiful people, we feel enriched. All of this outgoing, desire, and longing for union conjures the Greek god Eros. Struck by his arrow, our hearts feel a wonderful pain. Indeed, one of the myriad mines in the field of love is the danger of mainly loving our loving. Falling in love is so energizing, so uplifting and right, that it can seem an end in itself. The growing cadre of people who have many intense but short term affairs of the heart testifies to the reality of this danger. As their preoccupation with feeling rather than substance mounts, they become more and more pathetic, hollowed as though terminally ill.

Somewhat unwillingly, I once watched this process occur next door. A striking woman in her late thirties or early forties lived nearby. She was single, dressed beautifully, drove an expensive car, and entertained a daunting string of male visitors. This was not her profession. Weekdays she marched out faithfully to what seemed to be a good, executive job. But weekends, and not a few weeknights, she brought home young men, older men, big men, small men, cowboys, lawyer types, and many more. I know this because they would stagger past my window the next morning, as I scribbled in the early quiet. Hung over and needing a shave, they would retrace their way from the hunt's climaxes, clearly worn out by the fox.

As I saw one night at the symphony, the fox could be a very classy game. Poured into a stunning red dress, she prowled the intermissions on full alert. But, over time, even the fox grew weary. Her eyes sunk in their sockets, her makeup became heavier, and her skin tightened till she looked like a little monkey. By the time we moved out, I saw her as a soul strangely imprisoned. Beautiful, bright, surrounded with lovely things, she had become a little girl lost, a woman badly bruised.

That is my interpretation, of course, rooted in my view of eros. For those who think sexual love is free, unconnected to the rest of our selves, the reading might be very different. My reading depends on a very positive view of eros, in which it lodges at the center of our selves. What we love ardently determines most of what we become. Immediately, therefore, I would challenge any harsh disjunction between eros and agape. The love that the New Testament spotlights (agape) is indeed more self-sacrificing than eros, more filled with the Spirit that converts us to loving God and neighbor as ourselves. But it cannot be a love without passion or glowing joy, if my most godlike experiences have any validity. Consequently, I see the disjunctions that theologians sometimes make between eros and agape as products of a faulty anthropology. Against what I take to be the Catholic Christian view of human nature, this faulty anthropology so distrusts experience, so fears our strongest emotions, that it becomes blind to eros' great goodness. The love that the Song of Songs says is as strong as death has a huge dollop of eros. The love of many Christian mystics for their divine Lover is fulfilling ecstatically.

So, the glow that others set in our hearts, the fire great or small, is a form of love that Catholic Christianity baptizes. When your little child or your spouse looks so good to you that you could eat him up, you have nothing to fear from God. When you cleave to your lover in tenderness, and then violence, and then tenderness again, God takes no detour around your door. God is beautiful, and a lover of beauty. God desires both our love and ourselves, in his own inscrutable ways. The mystic ravished by God is no theological conundrum. The God desired by humans could be provocatively feminine. For too long we've put ropes around sexual love, made it an exceptional province. We are erotic because of how God has made us. We melt and rise up by God's divine choice. Let us praise this as we praise all our other endowments. As we find it good to have food and good to have sleep, let us find it good to have desire and good to have sex. Eros is god of more than sex, but sex is his deep penetration.

Intercourse

How to write about intercourse? It is so central and so holistic that it cries out for solid treatment, yet so personal that all treatments seemed doomed to failure from the start. When intercourse goes well, it both expresses love and builds it up, like our other sacraments. When it goes badly, it brings a special strain. We now lay so much burden on intercourse that it is bound often to fail us. In simpler times, things probably were more instinctive, though not necessarily more fulfilling, especially for a great many women. Today it seems we must learn a second naivete, practice to become easy and instinctive. So be it. Since the symphony is so important, rehearsal had best begin.[1]

When two people faithful to one another rehearse year by year, they become, as Paul saw, one body. Not just fleetingly, for their brief moments of sexual commingling. More and more perduringly, through longer and longer stretches of the day. What the other thinks, likely is suffering, probably would have to say, becomes a regular part of one's reflection. The other always remains other, a *difference* one wants vividly to live, yet becomes very much one's own.

The arithmetic is curious. Taken separately, John and Mary are two. In intercourse John and Mary are two conjoined, and so one in a significant sense. As lovers who regularly have deep intercourse, John and Mary become one and a half, the half being the *dimidium animae meae* of friendship, the other half of the friend's soul. As parents of Samantha, John and Mary are in part three. Jason, Cindy, Peter, and Bubb make them parts of four, five, six, and seven. How we are both ourselves and fractions of others is a set of puzzles worthy of Pythagoras or Gödel. And at the center of it, the four-dimensional nub, is the act of sexual intercourse, the font of biblical knowledge. Creative, it lets us increase and multiply. Imperative, it gives us our identity: why we leave father and mother, gain strength to work seven and then another seven years.

Intercourse is comforting, exciting, calming, educational. We can have too much of it, too little of it, times of plenty, and times of want. No act of intercourse is exactly like any other, yet all acts bear a family resemblance. The mystery of this deserves our best study, for we can learn, if we study well, a quite different way of being human. To enter is not the same as to be entered. To be small and strong can make fun of being large and weak. The corners of our dark glass can shift suddenly, bringing a kaleidoscopic flash of light. The constants are so simple we boggle every time we remember. Why don't we take more time? How have we become so frazzled? What keeps us from playing freely? When will our next perfection come?

Implicitly, such questions show the importance a holistic spirituality would place on intercourse. Next to prayer, which is our solitary or shared intercourse with God, sexual love-making is probably our most important spiritual activity. This is not to denigrate work, nor to deny that love includes sharing on many levels. It is simply to point out that the most whole of our bodily actions is our fullest fusion with the partner of our time, our fellow sojourner, the one who completes our analogy to Christ's union with the Church. For Paul, Christ was like a groom and the Church like a bride. They were married, united, compenetrated. Someday I would like to develop the reverse of this figure, taking God as the saints' lovely bride, but the overtones of the sexual roles matter much less than the drama on center stage: love suffuses being.

God would suffuse us with his being. God would be suffused with our being, little as it is. Between us and God there would be, if God had his way, no mine and thine, no withholding or divorce. God has his way in heaven, where the angels sing the nuptials of the lamb. There, in round, full intercourse, the Christ consummates all the espousals of time, all the love and grace that now can only be partial.

Feminism

When I confronted my stereotypes of promiscuity, and Paul's imagery for Christ and the Church, I ran into feminism, a potent factor on today's cultural scene. For a holistic spirituality, feminism is a blessing nearly unalloyed. At least eight of every ten feminist instincts or programs run in a holistic direction, cast off from partiality and divisiveness. Politically, most thoughtful feminists are socialists. Ecologically, most completely espouse conservation and a gentle symbiosis with nature. Economically, women's 59¢ dollar means joining together for deep change. Theologically, God the Mother is nurturing and full of feeling.

The separatist minority aside, feminists are one of our most precious columns of health. With blacks and other long-sufferers, they hold the key to our country's soul. Until we fully enfranchise women and people of color, we shall have no laudable revolution. What the colonies began in 1776 is still very much in labor. So too with what the Spirit began around 35 A.D. Until the feminine store of talents, insights, gifts, and needs graces all portions of the Church's table, the body will be somewhat sickly. Roman Catholic, Eastern Orthodox and evangelical Christians especially need to hear this part of what the Spirit is saying to all the churches.

In Dorothy Dinnerstein's stimulating book *The Mermaid and the Minotaur*,[2] one finds a laser-like focus on the female role in early child-rearing. Because early child-rearing has been an exclusively female preserve in most cultures, most human beings have gotten off to a stiff-gaited start. The Madonna/witch who personifies life's ambivalence has come from the face that dominated the cradle. As the source of the child's earliest pleasures and pains, the female has dominated its deepest psyche. Both the historical arrogation of worldly authority by men and the spiritual ambivalence of women have, in Dinnerstein's view, come from this earliest imbalance. Were men and women to share early child-rearing equally, more human beings might get off to a healthy start.

What Dinnerstein urges for child-rearing is but one example of the cultural changes that women's full liberation might entail. We have been without equal sexes so long that we don't really know what sexual equality would mean. Were women to have equal access to power in all the dimensions of human life, there is a chance that power would be less corrupting. Not because women are immaculately conceived or intrinsically virtuous. Because free women might lie and manipulate a great deal less, free men might be a great deal less windbaggy and rough-shod. Our male excesses of toughness have gotten us into nuclear and geo-political stalemates, while our female excesses of sweetness have trivialized millions of lives. Can there be a strength that does not bully, a nurturing that does not cloy? Obviously there can be. Enough mature, healthy men and women exist to model the wholeness we seek. But they are not so many that wholeness is the dominant vision. In all the major institutions of contemporary American culture—government, the military, academics, the Church, business, communications—wholeness is at best a glimmer, at worst not even wanted.

So there is a significant sense in which sexism is simple inhumanity, feminism is simply health. Not to be a feminist, in the sense of a champion of women's co-equal humanity, is to disserve the entire race. The lingering models of Aristotle and (part of) Paul that depict women as misbegotten males or the subordinate sex plague almost all pockets of our culture. Until they are cut out of our psyches like cancer, few of us will grow to full health. When the humanistic psychologist Abraham Maslow surveyed the American population a decade and a half ago, he found only the smallest fraction fully healthy, "realized" or close to whole. I think feminism has significantly increased the percentage of healthy women and men, but I'm not sure that even now we have reached double figures.

In good intercourse, sexual difference is utterly complemen-
tary. That is an interesting model. When the Bible speaks of God
creating humanity in the divine image and likeness, it notes that
"male and female he created them." Thus the image of God is
male-female, woman-man. So tight is the tie between theology
and anthropology that our deficient view of human nature has
deprived us of a full vision of God. For such a full vision, God
somehow is whole like a conjugal unit. That means God can give
and receive, love and be loved, go directly or obliquely. Glim-
mers of this flicker through the Christian tradition, especially in
ruminations on the Spirit, but we have a fresh opportunity to
catch the breeze and set full sail.

Beyond even the reforms needed in ecclesiastical politics lie
the reforms needed in our theological images. Let God start to
become what feminists sense in their most whole moments, and
a full new harmony might sound. For those with cross-cultural
earphones, it will recall the Chinese Tao or the Buddhist Prajna-
paramita (Wisdom-That-Has-Gone-Beyond). Both are subtle,
indirect, non-violent. Both bring forth many varieties of life.
Where violence ruins many human situations, both suggest the
patient procedures of nature, the power of time and tide. So both
feminine divinities live longer than the lesser martial gods. Both
become synonymous with beauty and grace. That is how our
Holy Spirit might be, were we to give voice to its current stir-
rings. Converted to images of wholeness, we might make charismatic power the majority party.

Marriage

Obviously enough, marriage is where feminism will have its
most profound impacts. Business, education, and politics will all
change, but the littlest dyad that gives us all life will be the most
crucial evolutionary carrier. What, then, ought we to be hoping
for marriage? How would a holistic imagination conjure its
future? The visions of artists such as Doris Lessing, whose novel
The Marriages Between Zones Three, Four, and Five[3] is a fascinating
meditation on male-female interactions, could stimulate good
theological phantasies.

Side by side, face to face, fitted like two spoons in a drawer, women and men of faith can play what Nietzsche considered the most dangerous game, immune from the poisons of Superman. Rejecting the image of the *Übermensch*, the male could take himself lightly. Refusing to choose between plaything and shrew, the female could engineer and waltz. The door is open, the God is limitless, the choices are none but our own. Certainly we will continue to be constrained by past practices, and certainly work and children will continue to take most of our pep. But, if we wish, we can have free zones for reconstruction. If we wish, the Spirit will suggest innovations, uprisings, or revolutions to make a new house a home.

Saturday morning, in a not so distant domicile, the phone rings to bring in the world. It is the Electrolux lady, calling to confirm delivery. That assured, she begins to explain assembly, storage, and diverse uses. The man finally shakes off his cobwebs, grasps the point, and realizes it's not his province. Assembly devolves to his woman. She is their maker and mover. Exit the man, enter the woman, adjust the caller as she can. The message is received, the lesson learned, and the machine begins its career of good service. For the marital couple themselves, it is just another little problem solved by judicious specialization. Each takes charge of what talent or training dictates. Both try to stretch so that they overlap, share, become as interchangeable as is useful. So he takes colors, she takes machines, and they divide up cooking and cleaning. He takes bills, she takes correspondence, and neither feels sorely burdened. The key to their good marriage is their collaboration.

Collaboration, patently enough, means working together. In this context, let it also imply working together *at* the marriage. As people change through their years, hoping to grow better and wiser, so their marriages change through the years, for better or for worse. As shrewd persons take some control of their change, trying to guide their work, friendships, prayer, and continuing education out of bootless channels, into lanes that profit, so the shrewd set of spouses take some control over their marital change, reviewing and redirecting it regularly. To do this—collaborate on their marriage, take some initiative over its direction—they must communicate what they are feeling, thinking, imagining. They don't have to communicate exhaustively every evening. They can't tear up the garden every weekend. But they should have some discussion most evenings, some focus most weekends on bed and board, money and service. His work, her work, the kids' needs, the kids' studies—that is the stuff of most marriages. Our task is to learn how to share them, to multiply their joys and halve their pains, without making our homes into igloos, structures rounded on themselves.

In today's high-powered Western culture, this is not an easy task. Many of the marriages potentially the richest soon grow frazzled and flat, because both spouses have overloaded their circuits. In a majority of middle class American homes, less would be a great deal more. Less material possessions and more space for quiet, music, or poetry. Less ambition at work or socially and more free time for reknitting and deepening the bond. Less running about and more hard exercise. Less eating and more pushing back from the table with a sigh of contentment. We've largely lost the art of gracious living, forgotten that the key is time.

Time is much more important to a good marriage than money. Granted enough money to get by in spare, simple fashion, money is usually superfluous, often a danger. Of greatest account is free time, regular chances to reconnoiter one's self, one's spouse, one's God. The quality of a good marriage is not strained. Like mercy, it flows and is resilient. So the pattern of many good marriages moves from isolation to dispersion to semi-isolation. Beginning immersed in one another, fused by their erotic attraction, the couple slowly extends itself into children, careers, friendships, causes, organizations. With the kids' leaving, however, a reflective, consolidating mood waves in. It is time to collect the pieces scattered hither and yon, to reglue the fragments and move on to a deeper level.

There a new motto presents itself: "A Few Things Well-Done." One or two sets of friends. One or two political causes. Time for polishing the silver, the sex, the liturgy. If our basic work is good, so that we earn our living digging new acreage for the kingdom, the rest of our time can increasingly become recreative. In the spirit of classical China, we can let retirement (the time away from work) become a Taoist haven: time for musing, reflection, listening to the music of the spheres. When they develop their contemplative selves, mature marital partners find numberless new perceptions to share. They consolidate their love, deepen their religion, and offer the next generation lessons in holism.

Defending Creation

In the consummating phases of many marriages, it becomes clear that God has given us sex as a prime weapon in the defense of all creation. Not only does sex give us new human life, it gives us much of the fostering, protective, ministerial attitude that life requires for its best prospering. When people use the creative powers closest to themselves well, they start out on a journey of protectiveness. Each partner to sexual love is vulnerable. Each needs considerateness and must give it. Made the basic charter of first a marriage and then a family, such considerateness can expand into work and civic life. The result can finally be the splendid virtue Erik Erikson saw at the end of the successful life-cycle: the wisdom to love life in the face of death.

It seems to me that this wisdom doesn't leap full-grown from the aged person's brow but builds slowly through previous experiences. Sexual love ordinarily moves to procreation, procreation leads to education, education takes the whole family into community projects and community projects open a window onto political life as a whole. This chain is not inevitable, but it has a certain strong logic and likelihood. If our love is to be generative, we must take responsibility for the large part of creation that comes under our influence, depends on us for its preservation and flourishing. The life of our lands and waters, of our infants and dying people, of our minds and souls is all somewhat in our hands. Instinctively, a holistic spirituality reaches out to nourish and protect this life, fighting against its destruction or death.

From this instinct certain political positions normally follow. Normally, the person well-centered in sexual love, well-aware of eros' implications, will stand against abortion, war, pollution, and social injustice of any stripe. The burden of proof will lie with any policy that seems to destroy life in the womb, promote the chances of war, further despoil the land or the people. There is room for discussion of almost all such policies, and strong need not to become monomaniacal, but inherent in most such discussions will be a call to consistency, so that one defends creation all along the line. Thus it makes little sense to be against abortion and for an arms buildup (the arguments for militarism being as slender as the trigger-finger of one madman). It makes little sense to work for clean air and tolerate economic policies that condemn ten percent of the work force to joblessness. If the official unemployment rate is ten percent, the real unemployment rate is closer to fifteen percent. Fifteen percent of one hundred million people is fifteen million people. If each jobless person is connected to two other people—spouse, children, or aged dependents—well over forty-five million people suffer. Politicians who shed tears for this horde on splendid mountain retreats have about them the smell of the crocodile.

Of course, one can make rhetoric from these things very facilely. In poetic silence a mere newscast can ignite rhapsodic rage. Much more significant is a solid determination: I shall stand against death. Calmly, knowingly, measuring the forces I resist, I shall try to be a peacemaker, a steward, a lover of creativity and compassion. What I learn joined to my spouse I shall apply wherever I can. The determination my eros gives, its steel for my soul, is a powerful opponent of death. Though the enemies of eros slay me, yet will I trust it, since it is a mark of my God. All creation is in labor for my God, and he will pay it fair wages. Come, Lord Jesus.

Chapter Nine
Education

Eros Again

The eros of our bodies manifests itself most strongly in sex. The eros of our minds manifests itself most strongly in artistic and scientific creativity, which ought to be the basic stuff of our education. Education clearly concerns any holistic regime, since it is the place we get many of the images and ideas that direct the rest of our lifetime. Therefore, a chapter on education.

If the health of an education shows in the popular culture its graduates love, American education currently needs a serious rehabilitation. Contemporary pluralism has so separated us from what used to be the perennial Western tradition that most of our people are confused and divided. They don't know how to put together science and art, or technology and religion, or ethics and politics. Everywhere one sees specialists, technicians in the pejorative sense. Almost nowhere does one see wise people modeling Aquinas' "sapientis est ordinare" ("It is the property of the wise person to bring things into order"). But without order there can be little wholeness.

I will skip the negative phenomenology, the exhibition of our current education's chambers of horrors. Suffice it to say that so many kids come to college (and leave college) unable to read, compute, analyze, communicate, and enjoy the life of the mind that any sane educator is bound always to be on the verge of depression. What most kids have missed, in my view, is intellectual eros. True, many of them also have missed basic grammar, vocabulary, and syntax, to say nothing of a sense of history and an exposure to international affairs. But these can all be remedied (the basic linguistic defects with more difficulty, the defects of exposure with less) if intellectual eros is aflame.

Intellectual eros is the simple desire to know. Classical Greek philosophy thought that all people by nature desire to know, and genetic psychologists such as Jean Piaget have confirmed this. Put in situations such as those that a Montessori school usually tries to create, children will be almost ravenous for learning. As with their appetite for food, they will gorge themselves and then withdraw to digest. But their feeding will be as steady and assured as an animal's in the forest, for they need to nourish their minds as surely as their muscles and bones. The delight they take in good food and good physical exercise parallels the delight they take in good learning. Indeed, to understand is a more thrilling experience, one of the key ecstasies that can redeem human finitude.

To understand, scientists will spend long, lonely years in antiseptic laboratories, patiently working away. The faintest lure of grasping the pattern, finding the key, will win their commitment to another full year's worth of labors. Of course scientists fantasize about winning Nobel prizes, gaining endowed chairs, being acknowledged as great benefactors of humanity. But these forms of recompense are extrinsic to the inner motivation of the genuine scientist, who is first of all a lover of understanding. In fact, unless understanding is its own reward, a scientist probably will fall on hard times, before long prostitute himself or herself for base gain. Relatedly, one striking index of a nation's appreciation of the human spirit is the support it gives basic research. When a nation pays more attention to technological applications than to basic scientific understanding, it has become both weak-witted and short-sighted. Over the long haul, nothing is more useful to a nation's technological advances than deepened understanding of nature's ground-level operations, and not to appreciate this is to show oneself terribly uneducated.

In the humanities, the social sciences, and the arts, eros takes somewhat different forms, but they all pivot on the by-play between imagination and active intellect. Creative understanding is grasping the intelligibility of something through a felicitous imagination of it. The scientists, artists, theologians, and sociologists who break open the next generation's worth of work are the few who imagine things freshly. Usually they have a solid grounding in the tradition of their discipline, combined with a strong sense of its inadequacies in face of the new era that is dawning. Thus poetic philosophers such as Nietzsche and Kierkegaard had studied the classical thinkers well, but they were almost soul-sick with an awareness that modernity had run the classical heritage into the ground. Nietzsche's Zarathustra and Kierkegaard's Johannes Climacus are alter-egos caught between the times. From the pain of being sorely squeezed, they brought forth dazzling images of what the spirit currently needed, messages straight from post-modernity's pre-conscious.

Granted, we are not geniuses like Nietzsche and Kierkegaard, Einstein and Freud, almost condemned to blaze pioneering paths. But almost all of us could be much more interested, involved, fired, and fulfilled than presently our educations have made us. Only a small number of us have challenging, demanding, holistic work that forces our minds to peak performance. Even in the university, where the pressures of marketing might be few, torpor far overbalances passion. At most schools, neither students nor faculty brim with intellectual eros. Consequently, both students and faculty feel hypocritical, as though only going through the motions. Sadly, many of them came with high hopes of catching a fire that would burn their lives long. By graduation or tenure the fire usually has burned down to a few flickering embers. Only the rarest student or teacher really believes that it could flare up again in a twinkling.

Scientific Research

Through science, intellectual eros gains discipline and precision. Its imaginative flights learn to carry payloads of logic and the criticism of evidence. The great gain in this educational process is boosting and spotlighting the power of explanation. A person brought up to scientific methodologies should be almost ruthless in demanding proof. The deeper scientist knows that this proof is not merely empirical, goes beyond a brute pointing to "facts." But facts or empirical evidence remains very important, like the "I'll believe it when I see it" of the person of sound common sense. Insofar as eros wants to know what is real, actuality rather than mere possibility, science gives it most valuable lessons. We owe the physiognomy of the modern world to empirical science, and much in that visage is admirable indeed.

Still, scientific training has its dangers, and too narrow an understanding of research can become an enemy of holism. Research scientists may so tunnel into their particular specialty that they resist the overtures their specialty itself may be making to collateral disciplines. Then one has the strange spectacle of people immersed in the study of an ecological nature refusing to admit the implications of nature's own holism. Such relatively new disciplines as bio-physics, bio-chemistry, socio-biology and the like show the breakdown of the old specialized tunnels. To gain fuller understanding, creative researchers have had to cut new connections.

Developments such as these do not abandon the scientist's drive to understand, his or her conviction that nature is amenable to rational investigation. They but bring to that drive and conviction a bit more sophistication and nuance. One can see the seeds of this sort of development in the reflections of Albert Einstein, who was passionately convinced that nature was intelligible through and through ("God does not play dice"), yet well aware of a mystery soliciting from the scientist instructive feelings, intuitive clues, some of them close to religious awe. Writing about religion and science, Einstein emphasized the "cosmic religious feeling" behind the scientists' labors, their passionate drive to understand: "I maintain that cosmic religious feeling is the strongest and noblest incitement to scientific research. Only those who realize the immense efforts and, above all, the devotion which pioneer work in theoretical science demands, can grasp the strength of the emotion out of which alone such work, remote as it is from the immediate realities of life, can issue.

What a deep conviction of the rationality of the universe and what a yearning to understand, were it but a feeble reflection of the mind revealed in this world, Kepler and Newton must have had to enable them to spend years of solitary labour in disentangling the principles of celestial mechanics."[1]

As his general essays show, Einstein was a fully cultured human being, interested in education, religion, and public affairs. Relativity in nature found a parallel in his own personal life: he could not keep his science sealed, cut off from the rest of his life. A generation later, the research biologist Lewis Thomas, president of Memorial Sloan-Kettering Cancer Center in New York, has been teaching medical doctors and amateur scientists holistic lessons drawn from a long career in the study of cells. Thomas lectured at Penn State University in the late 1970's while I was teaching there, and a portion of his lecture, reprinted in *The Medusa and the Snail,* has remained one of my best examples of the scientist's personal need for holism. Watching the play of otters and beavers at the Tucson Zoo, Thomas became aware of the losses that modern reductionism has inflicted on many scientists: "I was transfixed. As I now recall it, there was only one sensation in my head: pure elation, mixed with amazement at such perfection. Swept off my feet, I floated from one side to the other, swiveling my brain, staring astounded at the beavers, then at the otters. I could hear shouts across my corpus callosum, from one hemisphere to the other. I remember thinking, with what was left in charge of my consciousness, that I wanted no part of the science of beavers and otters; I wanted never to know how they performed their marvels; I wished no news about the physiology of their breathing, the coordination of their muscles, their vision, their endocrine systems, their digestive tracts. I hoped never to have to think of them as collections of cells. All I asked for was the full hairy complexity, then in front of my eyes, of whole, intact beavers and otters in motion."[2]

To keep in touch with the reality that dominates most human beings most of the time, to stay coordinated with the other horizons (artistic, religious, common-sensical) that interpret the world, scientists have to step back now and then as Thomas did and look at beavers, forests, solar systems, or members of their own species as wholes. The part can swell up to block the vision of the whole. Reductionism can become the dominant outlook. So a walk in the park or a night at the opera becomes a necessity for scientific balance. Like rocking a small child or attending to a student's personal pain, these little excursions help the researcher to remember, imagine, and think the world whole. He still has to narrow his focus to do certain kinds of very valuable work, but he has less danger of forgetting that this work is but one tile of an overall mosaic, a design so complex and vast we will always have more to love with our minds than all of them together could ever exhaust.

Humanistic Criticism

Somewhat parallel to scientific research is humanistic criticism, which also figures prominently in contemporary education. As scientists learn how to imagine experiments, gather data, and evaluate their findings probingly, so the historian or literary scholar learns to generate possible explanations, see what light they shed on new or old data, and subject them to rigorous criticism. What steps forth in both a scientific and a humanistic scrutiny is the reflective processes of judgment.

Whereas generating an hypothesis, pursuing a bright idea, is a matter of direct understanding, the processes that flash forth a sense of what *might* be, making good judgments, passing from hypotheses to solid theories, is a matter of surveying these direct processes reflectively, to see whether they finally hold up, really do allow one to say that something *is* so. The mature person makes a big distinction between what might be so and what actually is so. E.F. Hutton can talk all it wants about the stocks that might take off; it is the stocks that stand high when the bell finally sounds that actually prove themselves a good buy.

In humanistic circles these general observations recently have been pointed toward hermeneutics, the study of interpretation. Especially for scholars who deal with literary texts, the question of how best to extract a text's meaning has become very pressing. When one tries to answer this question, it quickly becomes clear that a text seldom has only one meaning. In addition to what the author originally may have meant (and that itself can be several-sided), there are the meanings that changed circumstances may suggest to a later reader, or the meanings that are simply innate, logical possibilities of the text itself. Thus there is no single interpretation of Sophocles' *Antigone*, Shakespeare's *Hamlet*, or the biblical Book of Job. Century by century, actor by actor, critic by critic, such classics reveal more and more possible meanings. So too with Alexander's campaigns, the Magna Carta, the American Civil War, or Mao Tse-tung's Long March. Literature and history admit of multiple interpretations, as do any other phenomena in which human beings are the central players. Even in theology, interpretation keeps developing new riches of possible significance. Thus David Tracy, a leading American Catholic theologian, has recently interpreted Jesus as the Christian "classic," the fontal source of Christianity that is a sort of living "text" for all the Christian generations.[3]

Along with this hermeneutical focus, of course, have come emphases largely determined by the interpreters' own upbringing or biases. One such emphasis comes through in what sometimes is called the "heremeneutic of suspicion." Under the influence of psychoanalysis, which has shown the complexity of human motivation, the large degree to which people may be unaware of the reasons they do many of the things they do, some scholars have come to take a negative, almost truculent attitude toward the matters they are to interpret. Arms folded across their chests, they face across the interrogation table and say to the poor little author or historical event, "Prove to me that you are innocent. Make the case that you mean what you say on the surface, are indeed moved by the motives you profess." No presumption of innocence here. The author is a criminal, the text is a fabrication, until strong evidence clearly proves otherwise.

So pictured, this description is probably a caricature, applicable to few actual humanists. But, like a cartoon, a caricature has the virtue of alerting us to distortions that are on the verge of twisting many "normal," business-as-usual situations. I think that this is now the case with the hermeneutic of suspicion. Having formed a generation's worth of humanists, it now shapes all sorts of academic, family, and church situations, in many cases to their detriment. The failures in collegiality that I sketched in Chapter Five relate to this issue directly. Suspicious, hypercritical, alert to every logical or motivational flaw, the professors in a majority of our universities' departments of English, history, philosophy, foreign languages, and, yes, religion tear down a great deal more than they build up.

Education, then, can become destructive. Where it ought primarily to flow from an eros responsive to beauty, lured by intellectual light, it can hunker down in the joys of demolition, the very ambiguous pleasures of battering weak structures apart. There is a place for demolition, of course, as there is a place for radical surgery. If an argument or an organ is rotten, the common good or general health may require us to cut if off. But this should not become our dominant, paradigmatic way of proceeding. When radical surgery becomes the instant recourse, the normal way of doing medicine, one has to guess that holistic values are being neglected, that quite suspect motives (financial profits, therapeutic ease, a mechanistic and unimaginative way of regarding patients) have come to hold undue sway.

The same in humanistic education. When students learn more about tearing Shakespeare apart than appreciating Shakespeare's splendid art, Shakespeare studies have gotten off the track. When the biblical vision is subordinated to philological criticsm or historical reductionism, biblical studies have gotten off the track. More generally, when students leave higher education better prepared to tear down than to build up, more suspicious than hopeful, the whole enterprise has misfired badly. Eros is a force for life, creativity, and joy, not death, dissection, and cynicism. Education is for making people whole, not alienating them from nature, society, themselves, or God.

General Education

When they try to address the misfirings of current higher education, academics often have recourse to tinkering with the curriculum. "Were we to provide a solid core of courses dealing with the basic materials," many say, "our students might emerge much better educated." The problem, though, is determining what those basic materials are and, even more, getting departments to drop their obsessions with turf and let a core curriculum function. Still, the movement toward a core curriculum or general education has much to commend it to a holistic spirituality. If students, or any of us, had the basic skills to educate ourselves ongoingly—the abilities to read, write, and compute; the ground level competence in the major disciplines: physical science, social science, mathematics, and literary studies—education would have much more sanguine prospects.

My main interest in this book, however, is not a philosophy of academic education. My main interest is the flowering of the love of God that invites us to become whole. How, then, might education best function in the life of people erotic for God's beauty, eager to know all they can know, as integratedly as they can know it, about God's reality? I think that it might best function in such a person's life existentially, as a specification of the mind's own dynamic tendency to make connections, build a more and more adequate world-view. Institutions must focus on such extrinsic aspects of education as curricula and credits. Spiritual theologians had better think hard before following their lead. The Spirit of God does not sigh too deep for words in any college catalogue. Only human minds and hearts draw the Spirit's interest to instruct. God's pedagogy is personal, existential, unique, tailored to what our genes and individual experiences have made us.

So, with all due respect to professors and deans, I would stress the educational process that actually makes people more whole: the reflection, reading, and research that construct the map of knowledge from within. Let me put this quite concretely. If a person set out to be, let us say, a musician, what educational process would I wish for him? It would be a process that (1) fired him with an eros of learning, and (2) showed him how to correlate things, make connections, and so feel that he would always have a dozen more things that he would like to study. Assuming that he had a real love of music, and some gifts, his music itself could be the center.

At the center, there would be lessons in an instrument: piano, violin, guitar. These presumably would whet his appetite, increase his desire to understand music more and more. Of course there would be patches of drudgery, seasons of drills and the mastery of basics. But a good teacher would assure that he received enough enjoyment from the development of his skill to keep him playing of his free volition. If he never played just for his own enjoyment, or for his family or friends, or with a little group at local gigs, the lessons would be going badly, the center would not long hold.

The center holding, one could add music theory, composition, and history. Thereby, "music" would start to swell, becoming not just the pleasurable thing that he experienced at the keyboard but one of humanity's immemorial treasures. It would connote the innovations of Bach, Mozart, and Beethoven. One could add the different styles of India, Africa, and East Asia. If the music really were to center an entire education (for this the student probably would have to follow a non-institutional, tutorial or self-directed program), it would lead on to mathematics and physics: How do harmonics work? What makes sound what it is? Next might come biology: How do we hear and play? Then psychology would be close at hand: Why is music pleasurable? From psychology one could step to philosophy: What does the musical imagination say about the mind in general?

I could fill in steps to theology, sociology, economics, and much more. Pedagogically, the point would always be the same: to use the student's practical interest, showing him that any of these studies was completely relevant: an explanation of an important dimension of the work centering his creativity. To be sure, I would hope that at some point the student would realize that economics, mathematics, or any of the other studies is valuable in its own right, interesting and explanatory because a significant expression of human intelligence. But the extrinsic approach to economics or mathematics—teaching them because they are objectively important—so often fails to engage students' interest that, had I a gifted and conscientious charge, I would do all I could to connect his studies with the work he most loved. So, be it music, theology, physics, or cabinet-making, I would labor hardest at helping him make the first delicate connections, experience the first flashes of relevance: "This explains part of the problem I'm having with the chair I'm building" (why teak is so hard, or so scarce, or should not be cut at these angles). Once we get educands to make connections, education starts to take care of itself.

The excitement I find in conceiving education this way, generally and holistically, is that it can meet us where we are right here and now. Whatever our age, job, or (within some limits) previous background, an educator possessed by intellectual eros, and aware of the disciplines' intrinsic connectedness, could sketch out a solid study program for any of us in less than half an hour. If we but told her the dominant interest in our life (sex, business, God, horses), and she knew her job, she could point to more relevant science, humanities, or religion than we could master in three lifetimes.

Example: Theological Studies

The love of learning that most directly relates to a holistic Christian spirituality is Christian theology. Therefore, let us consider how an ordinary person, striving to grow more whole through Christian faith, might develop a modest self-education in Christian theology.

Bernard Lonergan's *Method in Theology*[4] is perhaps the most adequate delineation of theology presently available, so let us use it to spotlight the parts of theology likely most useful to the ordinary person we have in mind. For Lonergan the scholarly enterprise of theology would become most collaborative (interdisciplinary and holistic) were it to coordinate eight "functional specialties." These are: research, interpretation, history, dialectics, foundations, doctrines, systematics, and communications. Research is the work that gathers and organizes the basic data: critical texts, archeological evidence, bibliographies, handbooks, maps, and the like. Interpretation is the work that reads out the meaning of these data. A prime example is the exegesis of scriptural texts: making clear what a Paul or John probably meant. History is the work that weaves such interpretations into an ongoing story of the Christian faith and community: how the meanings changed from the patristic to the medieval era, how

Augustine led on to Aquinas, what life was like in the Christian regime of John Calvin's Geneva. Dialectics is the work that adjudicates the debates over the different meanings that Christianity can have, as different historical reconstructions or philosophical points of view bring such differences to the point of clashing.

For Lonergan, these four functional specialties are theology's listening phase. If theology is to move from listening to speaking, building the Christian worldview afresh, it has to pivot and root the theologian's own consciousness in a vital commitment to Jesus. That is the process called conversion. Foundations is the functional specialty that expresses the theologian's Christian conversion, lays out the horizon that staking one's personal meaning on Jesus generates. With such an horizon, the doctrines of the Church make more sense, standing forth as the Christian community's official interpretation of how orthodox faith configures the world. Systematics is the specialty that tries to bring doctrines into the most coherent order possible. Relying heavily on the theologian's creative imagination, it begets such illuminating hypotheses as Thomas Aquinas' view that the center of the reality of Jesus Christ is the act of existence of the Eternal Word, or Karl Rahner's view that grace is ingredient in all people's lives as an "existential" or ever-operative factor. The last functional specialty, ideally flowing from a solid sense of the order of the whole, is communications: the effort to put the results of the process from research to systematics in the service of preaching, liturgy, catechetics, ethics, spirituality, and the other concerns of pastoral practice.

It seems clear to me that communications is the area that our ordinary person will find most profitable. Research is highly dependent on such special skills as ancient languages. Interpretation can be very germane, but only when it takes the time to express itself in general, everyday terms (speak as communications tries to speak). History, dialectics, doctrines, and systematics are quite similar: often relevant, but usually needing translation. Foundations regularly is more pressing and absorbing, because it stands so close to conversion, and because the best foundational theologians express their close contemplation of God's converting mystery in fresh, parabolic language. Still, foundations also can be difficult, so the theology usually of most use to the ordinary person is communications.

Look, then, for the biblical studies, doctrinal studies, historical studies, and systematic studies that seem to communicate most concretely and directly to your own interests: prayer, social issues, marriage, ecology, education or whatever. Insofar as they lead you to want to know more about Scripture itself, or Church history itself, or ecclesiological doctrine itself, you might try more specialized studies, verge closer to scientific works in their area. But make them serve your own predominant interest. Like the musician moving from the center of his creative work to a physics or psychology that illumines it, ask theology to relate to your current interests, passions, problems.

For example, if you are torn apart by a divorce, let this trauma become a stimulus to study the history of Christian teaching on divorce, investigate what progressive systematicians are now making of it, look into what new exegesis of the classical New Testament texts is suggesting. Or see whether the several organizations dealing with the problems of Christian divorce haven't generated suggestions for liturgies on this theme, how to pray about this problem, how to keep a warm sexuality alive. Theological studies should be the educational side of your personal faith. They should feed your personal intellectual eros that wants to be purified by God's eros, God's ardor that human beings become fully alive. That was how the Greek Father Irenaeus thought of God's glory. To shine with a full manifestation of his splendor, God needed human beings fully alive: healthy, energetic, curious, creative, passionate, humble, and joyous. Theological studies above all should augment our joy. Focusing on the best of all subjects, the Father of Lights from whom every good gift descends, they should firm our minds and warm our hearts, communicating the best that our long tradition has learned about the ordinary pedagogies of the Spirit.[5]

Chapter Ten
Meditation

Eastern Regimes

Theological studies once furnished Christians intellectually alive the main substance of their personal spiritual lives. For the Fathers of the Church, East and West, there was little divorce between prayer and study. The advent of scientific theological studies, sophisticated to the degree of models such as Lonergan's, has left the personal significance of theology somewhat ambiguous. In foundations and communications, as we noted, the personal quotient is large, but it is easy in the other specialties to study as though the text were thermodynamics. As a result, we have a heightened need for Christian exercises that nourish the deeper part of the mind, feed the heart, take us to the ground of our spirits. In this chapter we consider some such exercises, under the general rubric of "meditation."

The religions of India and East Asia, which Christian spiritual theologians are now studying with great interest, have developed rich treasuries of wisdom about meditation. Very quickly, one studying the meditational regimes of Hinduism or Buddhism, Taoism or Confucianism, finds that they are *analogous* to Christian spiritual regimes: somewhat like, and somewhat different. The likeness roots in their effort to focus the mind and discipline the spirit—collect the person, center him down, put him in touch with his truest self and ultimate reality. The difference roots in the generally impersonal character of the Eastern ultimate reality (there are large exceptions to this statement) and (to a lesser extent) in the sort of detachment that the Eastern sages usually recommend. Nonetheless, the analogies from Eastern yogins and sages are sufficiently striking to stimulate many useful Christian reflections.[1]

Consider, for example, the opening lines of the *Dhammapada*, a little portion of the Buddhist canon much beloved throughout all Buddhist lands:

> What we are today comes from our thoughts of yesterday, and our present thoughts build our life of tomorrow: our life is the creation of our mind. If a man speaks or acts with an impure mind, suffering follows him as the wheel of the cart follows the beast that draws the cart. What we are today comes from our thoughts of yesterday, and our present thoughts build our life of tomorrow; our life is the creation of our mind. If a man speaks or acts with a pure mind, joy follows him as his own shadow. "He insulted me, he hurt me, he defeated me, he robbed me." Those who think such thoughts will not be free from hate. For hate is not conquered by hate: hate is conquered by love. This is a law eternal.[2]

It would be hard to find a simpler, more effective presentation of the influence that our thoughts have on our personalities. If today's nutritionists can say that we are what we eat, because they know the great influence that such somatic ingredients as minerals and proteins can have on our psyches, yesterday's spiritual masters could say, with even more warrant, that we are what we think: Our personalities are largely the meeting ground of our loves and hates. For Buddhist masters, convinced of the Buddha's First Noble Truth ("All Life Is Suffering"), the person (we bracket the issue of the Buddhist teaching of *anatta*, which holds that there is no self or person) whose mind is impure or filled with wrongful desire is bound to suffering like a beast to a cart. The (karmic) tie between desire and suffering is iron-clad, inevitable. Conversely, the person of pure or detached mentality equally inevitably comes into rich measures of joy. Consequently, Buddhist meditation masters tried to exercise their charges in detachment. "Get rid of all those broodings about the injuries done you," they counseled. "Move yourself from hate to love. That is the way to freedom and happiness. That is how you can gain the Enlightened One's serene contentment."

It is not hard to see that the *Dhammapada* remains a contemporary text. Indeed, in season and out, in the medieval university and the modern banking center, the message of the Dhammapada has been relevant: How you manage your mind is the key to your mental health. Hindu yogins and East Asian contemplatives would largely agree: The world is a function of how we regard it; our peace or distress is mainly up to ourselves. Against the modern Western tendency to try to change things from without, by new economic or political arrangements, the East has stressed the change that must occur within, through quiet but vigorous meditation.

Perhaps even more influential than the *Dhammapada* has been the *Tao Te Ching*, a Chinese text of similar brevity and power from about 300 B.C. Almost any chapter of the *Tao Te Ching* will echo the lessons of the *Dhammapada*, with the slightly different overtone that inner harmony is nature's own way. Following nature's way *(tao)*, the sage would offer teachings such as this: "Your name or your person, which is dearer? Your person or your goods, which is worth more? Gain or loss, which is a greater bane? That is why excessive meanness is sure to lead to great expense; too much store is sure to end in immense loss. Know contentment and you will suffer no disgrace; know when to stop and you will meet with no danger. You can then endure."[3]

Practical, ethical, concerned with helping us come to self-control and contentedness, the Eastern meditational classics remain an invaluable part of all humanity's spiritual heritage. Christians interested in becoming whole should not neglect them, for the one God who has not left himself without trace anywhere moves over their quiet waters.

Psychoanalysis

A major difference between our minds and those of the authors of the *Dhammapada* and the *Tao Te Ching* is our current awareness of unconscious motivations. True, teachers experienced in the interior life have always known that the psyche has many strange aspects, but only with Freud and his psychoanalytic successors have we begun to take this irrational realm into account generally, throughout the culture at large, and systematically, through theories of psychodynamics. This awareness impinges on meditation, of course, making it suspect for many people. Is prayer anything more than talking to ourselves? Is meditation anything more than taming our psychic energies?

The answer to the first question depends on our convictions about God. If we are peaceful in the Christian conviction that God is the independent Creator of the world, that Jesus is risen and fully alive, that the Spirit breathes where he will, then praying to God will not seem egocentric or self-deceptive. The goal of Christian meditation, as somewhat distinct from Eastern meditations, is loving communion with an objective God. The Christian exercises of pondering scriptural texts, thinking about doctrinal truths, picturing Gospel scenes, or examining one's recent conduct are all but way-stations to the goal of Christian interiority, which is loving intercourse with the Creator. Conceived as personal, the Christian God is an "other" fit for conversation, able to be spoken to and heard from. As Christian prayer develops, waiting for God's word can become the dominant motif. But at any stage the conviction remains that the opaque mystery of God is objective, beyond and more than the meditator's self. Indeed, for Christian spiritual theology Jesus had an historical reality, was present at a definite period of time in a definite patch of space, as though to cap the objectivity of the Christian God and show in an especially concrete way that "God" is not just the self's projection.

Concerning the relation between meditation and the taming of our psychic energies, some remarks of Roshi Philip Kapleau, a contemporary Zen master, may be illuminating:

> In the psychophysical therapies meditation is essentially a means to attain relaxation and to quiet random thoughts so that one functions more effectively on a psychophysical level. But when meditation is not fueled by the desire for religious awak-

ening and is divorced from the teaching that no man is an
island unto himself, it can easily degenerate into a self-satisfied
numbness to the pain of others. In his article entitled "The
New Narcissism" [*Harpers*, October 1975] Peter Marin comes
down heavily on the trend in therapy toward what he calls
"the deification of the isolated self," and speaks of the "ways
in which selfishness and moral blindness now assert themselves in the larger culture as enlightenment and psychic
health. . . . " My own experience conducting workshops at the
invitation of encounter and therapy groups would tend to bear
out Marin's contentions.[4]

For Zen, therefore, the goal of meditation is not merely the
sublimation or pacification of psychic energies or other sources
of inner turmoil. The same with Christian meditations. They
may indeed bring the person to joy and peace, but that will be
as an effect, an overflow of reaching their main goal: uniting the
person to the holy God. In neither Zen nor Christian meditation
does one lose the world. The way in becomes the way out. A
clarity of vision, balance, good humor, and hard-headed realism
attend both the Zen and the Christian masters. They don't bother
to dispute the findings of psychoanalysis. Whatever illumines
the workings of the psyche can be helpful. But their goal is simpler and more profound: grasping ultimate reality, moving
beyond the punishments and seductions of the immature or
wounded psyche to firm yet supple interactions with things as
they really are.

So meditation subjects the hermeneutic of suspicion that I
mentioned earlier to a considerable tempering. Aware of psychoanalysis' map of the psyche, the religious meditator takes a wry
look at his or her own motivation, and the motivation of others,
but refuses to let himself or herself turn sour. True, what fools
these mortals be! Yet God has made them little less than angels.
The grace of God is more beautiful than the ugliness of our toady
unconscious. The path of growth is a detour around the cynical
thoughts and advice that would cripple us. This does not mean
a hermeneutic of optimism. We don't have to interpret everything like Pollyanna. It ought to mean a hermeneutic of hope:

interpreting everything as though it were less important, less powerful, less decisive than God's love.

One of the key moments in the religious life is when we freely choose to make our hermeneutic Christian. Thenceforth, we try to interpret all our experiences in the framework of a good news established once and for all, bound never finally to fail. This Christian hermeneutic has to become quite sophisticated, learning to discern the Spirit of God from the spirits of false consolation. But it entails a relativizing of most of the "evils" that upset irreligious meditators. The mystery of God can absorb great amounts of anxiety. The Christian meditator comforted by the Spirit into maturity abandons large portions of self-concern. God must increase. We must decrease. We are not what is important. The overall pattern and plan of God is what is important. So we can be free—much less conflicted, neurotic, narcissistic. Letting false worries slip away, taking real worries directly to our Source, we can capture a solid measure of mental health, enough to help us work and love fruitfully.

Western Regimes I

Those who wish to aim at becoming more able to work and love fruitfully, connected with the divine Spirit, need not take themselves to esoteric gurus. The staple teachings of the mainline Christian masters are completely adequate to this goal. If one feels the need for spiritual direction, or wants to investigate imaginative amalgams of the Eastern and Western traditions, well and good. Spiritual direction can be a great aid, and imagination is usually a great boon.[5] But such staple teachings as those of Ignatius Loyola's *Spiritual Exercises* and the anonymous *Cloud of Unknowing* furnish plenty of food for holistic development. The variety of methods they propose, and the depth of experience they indicate, have made them spiritual classics. In my opinion, one always does well first to visit the classics.

The *Spiritual Exercises* have been the dominant force in modern Roman Catholic spirituality. This is not to denigrate Benedictine, Dominican, or Franciscan spirituality. It is not to deny the great influence of *The Imitation of Christ*. It is simply to agree with the prevailing impression that modern times demanded more mobile, active sorts of ascetical and mystical regimes, and that Ignatius Loyola furnished their paradigm. His work was biblical and traditional yet profoundly original. Stemming from his own experiences of conversion and sublime union with God, the *Spiritual Exercises* carry the ring of authenticity. People who have made the full month of the *Exercises* seldom have emerged unchanged. So intense a light does Ignatius shine on the Christian faith, so powerful a dialectic of the energies of repentance and commitment does he forge, that those who go through the Exercises find themselves brought face to face with Christ untamed.

The four "weeks" of the *Exercises* lay out the main movements of Ignatius' dialectic. First there is the foundational view of Christian spirituality: we are creatures and sinners. Almost ruthlessly, Ignatius takes away all the hovels in which we would hide from the first truths of our condition. Of ourselves, we are nothing. Completely, we depend upon God's gratuitous love. If this is true regarding our existence, it is even more true regarding our salvation. By turning our backs on God, dilly-dallying with various apathies or actively fostering disorder, we have denied our status as creatures, imitated Lucifer's "I will not serve." Rising up on our hind legs, we have tried to block out the sun that gives all creation its light, the mystery that must overcome death if we are not to live meaninglessly. In the beginning of any profound spiritual regime, therefore, lies the moment of conversion. Until we turn away from our dreaming, get the realities of our situation straight, we will make no solid progress.

Second, there is the illumination that the evangelical Christ offers. To follow Jesus through the Gospels, watching his teaching, healing, and prayer to the Father, is to activate one's supposed faith that he is the Word Incarnate, the living symbol of God's creativity. For the alert Christian, the main modality of the spiritual life will always be an imitation of the Christ. As Jesus bore himself toward God, and toward his fellow humans, so have all the Christian saints. The love that Jesus showed, the power and compassion, remain the prime exemplar of what God wants to do with us other images and children. Prescinding from such accidentals as Jesus' dress, sex, and cultural conditionings, the alert Christian rivets on to the heart of the Christian matter, Jesus' amazingly fertile love.

The third week of the *Exercises* takes one to the depths of this fertile love. Contemplating Jesus' sufferings and death, Ignatius drives home the point that all this endurance and pain was *for me*. Existential long before his time, Ignatius rivets Christ's passion onto the exercitant's own person. This was not a casual historical happening. This was the event in which the horror of my sins and the ardor of God's love for me fused in bloody combat. If I want to see what human malice can do to God, I need only regard Christ crucified. As a metaphor for all human suffering, Jesus gathers together the passion of a very wayward history. But the embrace into which he takes our sufferings crushes the evil in us and our world like a bear snapping his enemy's spine. God is the strong one and Satan the weak. Where sin abounded, God's grace has abounded the more.

So the forth week of the *Exercises* takes one to the heights of God's fertile love. Jesus crucified becomes Jesus resurrected. Dying he destroyed our death, rising he restored our life. Henceforth, he lives at the right hand of God, making our world more congenial than threatening. To be sure, we need strong eyes of faith to see this. The Spirit is subtler than Satan, a worker of substance rather than superficialities. But the "Contemplation To Obtain Divine Love" with which Ignatius climaxes the fourth week shows a vision of the world shot through with God's love, bearing God to us in every nook and cranny. The staples of Christian meditation—thinking about faith's propositions, imagining Jesus' sayings and doings, slowly repeating venerable prayers, examining one's conscience for signs of accepting or rejecting the Spirit, resting quietly in God's darkness or embrace—all these are in the order of means, as good or bad as honest trial finds them. The order of ends is the ongoing process of conversion, illumination, confronting Jesus' death, and embracing Jesus' resurrection that the *Exercises* expose with a classical economy and depth.

Western Regimes II

I am aware that wooden exposition of Ignatius' various "points" for meditation has often brought the *Exercises* into contempt. All praise, therefore, to the critics and reformers who have helped to bring out the mystagogic, evocative substance of Ignatius' masterpiece.[6] The truths of our creaturehood, sinfulness, Gospel call to follow Christ, implication in Christ's passion, and liberation by Christ's resurrection will never move far from the center of an authentic Christian spirituality, but we should re-express then freshly generation by generation. Thus depth psychology may suggest a new imagery to replace Ignatius' good and evil spirits. Ecological studies may fill out the implications of sin and creaturehood. Jesus' speech, so lively and teasing, may suggest poetic approaches to Christology. The sufferings of modern history may place Jesus' passion and resurrection in bolder relief. Classics are not classics because they have said the final word, imprisoned language so that we can never add new imagery. Classics are classics because of their depth. A work like the *Exercises* goes so deeply into Christian religious experience that it is always relevant—if we ourselves are deep enough to appreciate Ignatius' charisms.

The case is much the same with other classics, such as the *Cloud of Unknowing*. Rooted in the "negative" theological tradition, which stresses God's distance from all our images and concepts of him, the *Cloud* yet makes such positive, simple, and attractive proposals for Christian meditation that centuries of Christian seekers have found it a wonderful resource. Recently it has figured in the movement to develop a "centering" prayer that tries to help people tie themselves to God center to center.[7] Using our affections, we can travel into God's mystery, going places our mind can never map. By simple exhalations and inhalations of love, or the rhythmic recitation of a mantra such as "Jesus" or "Have mercy," we can slowly come to rest in God, open the roof of our consciousness to God, deal simply with the utter divine simplicity. Then we may experience how we are concentric with God.

The main point of the *Cloud* parallels the main point of the classical Spanish mystic John of the Cross: to advance toward union with God, real-ize something of what and who God is, we must be purified of the sensual and spiritual obstacles we possess, or erect, or indulge. For the *Cloud*, people who have pondered the Christian teachings, and made a good effort to lead morally upright lives, stand a good chance of being led by the Spirit toward such real-ization. If they persist in praying regularly, they likely will find themselves dissatisfied with their many words, thoughts, ruminations. These are all partial, fragmentary, unequal to the wholeness of the self they want to offer, the God they want to love. So they may, if they are fortunate enough to receive the traditional contemplative counsel, let go of such relatively superficial spiritual concerns and try to abide in simple unknowing.

As the dominant symbol of the *Cloud* suggests, God always overshadows our minds. To be real for us God must appear as a darkness, a no-thing-ness. We mistakenly think that this darkness is a nothingness, a void, a pure absence. But, as Pascal saw, we would not seek God had we not already found God. We wouldn't sense God as an absence if we didn't know, at least in anticipatory, proleptic fashion, something of God's presence. From the light that flashes when we understand, we intuit that God must be light in which there is no darkness at all. The *Cloud* would have us go on to realize that for us this divine light is bound to appear as darkness. God is too bright, too vast, too deep for us to comprehend. The best thing we can do is abide in God's dark presence, letting our love be our whole conversation.

Eastern Orthodoxy, of course, has been greatly influenced by this negative tradition, which it usually traces back to Denis the Areopagite.[8] Lost in the mystery of the Trinity, Eastern contemplatives yet have come forth with splendid icons of Jesus and Mary, profound practices such as the Jesus Prayer. Simply by repeating "Lord Jesus Christ, have mercy on me, a sinner" night and day, many Eastern contemplatives have slowly identified their lives, their selves, with Jesus, so that waking or sleeping they lived, now not them, but Christ Jesus in them. "Unknowing," then, is no enemy of intimacy with Jesus.

Mother Alexandra, a contemporary hegumena or abbess living in Pennsylvania, describes how this union worked out for her:

> The Jesus Prayer can be used for worship and petition; as intercession, invocation, adoration, and as thanksgiving. It is a means by which we lay all that is in our hearts, both for God and man, at the feet of Jesus. It is a means of communion with God and with all those who pray. The fact that we can train our hearts to go on praying even when we sleep keeps us uninterruptedly within the community of prayer. This is no fanciful statement; many have experienced this life-giving fact.... I had a most striking proof of uninterrupted communion with all those who pray when I lately underwent surgery. I lay long under anesthesia. "Jesus" had been my last conscious thought—and the first word on my lips as I awoke. It was marvelous beyond words to find that although I knew nothing of what was happening to my body I never lost cognizance of being prayed for and of praying myself. After such an experience one no longer wonders that there are great souls who devote their lives exclusively to prayer.[9]

Mysticism

At this point we have come to at least the borders of mysticism strictly so called. People such as Mother Alexandra appear to be "patiens divina": directly experiencing God's influence. Such an experience is entirely God's doing. The most that the individual can do to prepare himself for such intimacy with God is to purify his motivation and try to follow the Spirit's lead into "acquired contemplation."

Acquired contemplation is a form of prayer in which one regularly is peacefully absorbed with God, either in an imageless way like that suggested by the *Cloud*, or by a holistic focus on Jesus, one of the Gospel scenes, a beautiful garden that seems pregnant with God's presence, or the like. The way to such a prayer seems to be to remain faithful to one's chosen periods of prayer, and sensitive to the Spirit's leadings, so that the Christian worldview more and more becomes one's own and produces feelings of being reformed, cured, made whole. Prayer is a time of spiritual nourishment. Many of its sensations are analogous to feeding. Slowly, we should find our innermost selves feeling better—stronger, wholer, more capable of doing the good we would do and resisting the evil we would not have prosper. An acquired, regular prayer in which we commune with the divine mystery or Jesus simply, heart to heart, can be an immense help to becoming full grown.

Such a description remains substantially true even through times of trial: dryness, discouragement, distraction, dividedness. The person faithful to prayer becomes involved in a process of transformation, some periods of which will almost surely be painful. For example, likely there will be a need to confront how superficial one often has been in the past. There likely will be a need to realize that God does not keep his people from sufferings. At some point the cross of Christ probably will become more than an extrinsic emblem. At work as well as at prayer, one may have to make leaps of faith, almost force the Christian interpretation of things to hold by sheer will power. At such times, biblical passages like Exodus 3, where God suggests that we learn the divine nature by sojourning with his mystery through time, and Romans 8, where Paul describes the help of the Spirit eloquently, can be a great comfort. Take courage, they say, Jesus has overcome the world—even the world in our own hearts, the part of our very selves that opposes love's rule.

If we are to develop modes of prayer suitably holistic and contemporary, probably we are going to have to take the Spirit's help, the experiential nature of our covenant with God, more seriously than past theology has encouraged the Christian laity to do. Probably, in fact, we are going to have to make mysticism a central topic in Christian theology. Were we to do this, we would follow the advice of Karl Rahner, perhaps the most influential Roman Catholic theologian of the past generation, who has labored mightily to mend the split between mystical and systematic theology that modernity created:

Karl Rahner is one of the few theologians of this century to give serious consideration to the mystics and their writings as valuable theological sources. The mystics do theology, for Rahner, because they teach "something about mysticism." The *Spiritual Exercises*, and other mystical classics, for example, are important because they are a "creative prototype . . . [and] a subject of tomorrow's theology." The great mystics, moreover, present a paradigm, a clarification, and an illumination of what takes place everywhere in faith, hope, and love. We see more clearly and explicitly in their lives what is taking place in the lives of all persons of good faith. Rahner stands, therefore, as a critical corrective both to the Continental Protestant tendency to dismiss mysticism as heresy and to the traditional Catholic isolation of mysticism from the other areas of theology. These are only a few reasons why Rahner has chided his fellow theologians for their lack of interest in mystical questions.[10]

The mystics illumine "what takes place everywhere in faith, hope, and love"—that is the sentence I'll like to gloss. We all have a capacity for God, since we all are restless spirits seeking the divine light and love. We all feel the lure of God's grace, since God has not left himself without witness anywhere. Consequently, we all are engaged in a dialogue, collaboration, process of agreement with God and resistance to God, because "God" is the mystery at the heart of, coincident with, our very humanity. To have faith that life is worth continuing, hope that justice one day will prevail, love for even those who are very hard to like is the sort of revelatory activity that spotlights our coincidence with God. The center from which such "theological virtues" flow recedes out of our sight.

We rest on an ocean of being that we cannot sound. Pain and joy, grief and ecstasy, drama in the theater or banality at home all can carry God's touch, because God fills the world, is the very milieu in which spiritual beings live and move and have their being. Therefore, to become more whole in one's Christian faith is virtually the same as becoming more whole in one's simple personhood. The sensitivity, strength, awareness, creativity, self-sacrifice and the like that signal a special "humanity" are the marrow of ordinary mysticism and holiness. So Paul could tell the Philippians, "Let your magnanimity be manifest to all. The Lord is near; have no anxiety, but in everything make your requests known to God in prayer and petition with thanksgiving. Then the peace of God, which is beyond our utmost understanding, will keep guard over your hearts and your thoughts, in Christ Jesus. And now, my friends, all that is true, all that is noble, all that is just and pure, all that is lovable and gracious, whatever is excellent and admirable—fill your thoughts with these things" (Phil 4:5–8).

Chapter Eleven
Theological Reflections

Evil

We began the arc of our holistic considerations, in Chapter One by dealing with theological horizons. God's love, a central focus in any theology, took us to nature, society (economics, politics, and grass-roots communities), and several realms of the self (diet and health, exercise and play, sexuality, education, and meditation). Now, to complete the circle, we return to theological considerations. Do the hopeful views that we derived from Christian faith finally stand up? If we generalize the troublesome, recalcitrant portions of experience that we have seen, can we finally gauge the place of evil and suffering, forgiveness and grace? When all is said and done, is Jesus' twofold love a realistic program for wholeness? Are we personally persuaded that this love best empowers a holistic life? What, indeed, might a day in the life of a holistic Christian look like? What simple practices might make our theories work? These are the sorts of questions we reflect upon in conclusion.

We have seen evil at all the stops on our journey. Today's ecological crises bear the smudge of human disorder and greed. Our economic, political, and social disorders point back to people not fully in love with God, not willing to love their neighbors as themselves. Most of us resist common sense in what we eat and drink, how we run our bodies, how we provide for beauty and poetry. Many of us share our culture's sexual disturbances, so that our most intimate love does not bear the joy and increase it ought. By and large our education has left the path of wisdom and wholeness, becoming blinkered in specialization. Most contemporary Americans therefore know little about the working of their minds, pray and meditate badly. The overall result is lives much more hurtful, much less mystical, than God intended. On bad days the enemies of wholeness seem a vast horde poised to sweep down on a darkling plain.

From trivial distraction to diabolical hatred, evil is God's enemy. Not only do disordered movers and shakers slash at human happiness, they shake their fists at God. Dachau, the Gulag Archipelago, the torture cells of Latin America, and the tiger cages of Vietnam are obscene twistings of the human spirit. The spawn of spastic souls, they try to snuff the human being's last flame, the hope that God does prevail. But that hope proves surprisingly strong. Only the few people who enjoy doing evil, and who no longer feel that torture and murder are wrong, do not remain God's allies, witnesses to how things ought to be. Indeed, it is almost impossible not to be God's ally, as the reaction of even evildoers themselves usually proves. Not only do most evildoers try to cover their actions with a facade of respectability, they shout with pain when they themselves suffer violation. So Stalin and Hitler mounted great propaganda campaigns to put a smooth face on their grotesque evils. So few Nazis or other criminals have not sweated and protested when they themselves had to mount the rack.

The fact of the matter is that God has made the world so that it opposes evil. Evil is non-being, disorder, lovelessness, the will to hurt and destroy. It has no positive, independent existence. We only perceive non-being or disorder as a crack or warping in being or coherence. Thus God, the fullness of being, prevails over chaos or the void. Thus the marvel of such a complex "system" as New York City is not the thousands of things that go wrong each day but the millions of things that go right. For ten million people to survive, and only some thousands to die, or some hundreds to be victimized by crime, suggests that evil is the lesser power. That hardly makes New York City a model of sane human living, but it shows that the headlines are far from the most basic news.

One can make similar analyses of lovelessness and the will to hurt. Everywhere people receive less than the full measure of love that ideally they would. In many places spiritual malnutrition breaks out in ill will and violence. Yet, most children smile, most neighborhoods manage, most jobless people keep trying. Worldwide, we do have enormous basic problems, billions of people do suffer much more than they should. Worldwide, our economic and political systems do reek of godlessness. Nuclear arms and industrial pollution threaten to bury us. Distributive injustice is almost as pervasive as original sin. However, more persuasive to most people than nuclear arms and industrial pollution are scenarios of peace and clean air. We may not have the full will to enact these scenarios, but most of us know without hesitation that they are the part of health. Vulnerable as we are to massive evil effects from small miscalculations or malevolences in areas such as nuclear arms or nuclear radiation, the vote of almost all our people is for letting one another alone, strolling near restful waters.

The most healthy response to evil, then, is resistance. In spirit one says, "No, this should not be!" In body, mind, and community, one does what one can to make such a judgment practical, defend the realm of health. As long as there remains stout resistance to evil, as for example in labor unions like Solidarity, the light still shines in the darkness, the darkness still fails to comprehend.

Suffering

The Greek dramatist Aeschylus had it that wisdom comes through suffering. In a world of finitude and sin, we are bound to meet resistance, failure, pain, and defeat. Some of this suffering will come by statistical probability: cancer, heart attack, car accident, flood. More will come from human factors such as stupidity and greed. Spiritually, however, the point is less the origin than our response. What do we make of the times that go wrong, the spaces needing redemption? How do we stir up our faith, become seconders of Paul's credo that *nothing* can separate us from the love of God in Christ Jesus?

First, by noting the ethical choice implicit in Paul's credo. The love of God in Christ Jesus was Paul's whole treasure. For Paul to live was Christ and to die was gain. The consolations of Paul's credo depend on this ethical choice. If something other than the love of God in Christ Jesus holds sway in our hearts, we are bound to find the assurances of Christ's Spirit problematic. And, of course, almost always, the blandishments of mammon lure us; we want to look good in the eyes of the world.

So, at the beginning of a spirituality holistic enough to hold off evil, and to help suffering become the purifier it should, lies a powerful dose of *detachment*. Daily, we must pray for bread and forgiveness, the grace to let *God's* will prevail. With such grace, we can halve whatever sufferings the day brings. Clutching fewer false ambitions, we can stand free of many heartaches. Rich people find it hard to enter the kingdom of heaven because often they are laden with many objects of desire, causes of spiritual sadness. The kingdom of heaven is among us as a power that dispels spiritual sadness, opens spaces of freedom and joy.

Second, we can move toward Paul's great confidence by bearing simply, manfully, the pains we cannot avoid, the evils other people do us. Take, for example, a man suffering a physical debility—angina from arterial congestion. Not only does this worry him, it worries his whole family. Physically, he may do all that he can to improve his condition: follow his doctors' suggestions, eat sensibly, get good exercise, avoid unnecessary tensions. Spiritually, he may still have to manage a sizable load of emotions: fear, guilt, resentment, regret. What if the sharp pains should come again tonight, when tomorrow he especially needs a good performance? Why should his wife have to carry such worries? It isn't fair that other people should enjoy good health effortlessly, oblivious even to their good luck. If only he had lived sensibly when he was young, not smoked and stuffed himself.

Most of this emotional turmoil is fruitless, but little of it turns off like the radio. So the man must learn to be patient with himself, accept his inclinations to agitation, move to the depths of his spirit where he can surrender himself to God, to be done with as God's goodness desires. Progress in this direction may be very slow. Success in self-management is always chancy, a day by day affair. One learns that peace today does not guarantee peace tomorrow. One realizes that two steps forward and one step back is an excellent pattern indeed.

Religiously, the man probably would be most helped by acknowledging his suffering. For God's ultimately mysterious reasons, he is vividly experiencing the imperfections of creation, things that ideally should not be. But so did Christ experience the imperfections of creation, the painful conjunction of necessity and folly. That Christ was innocent and the man knows he is not doesn't remove the essential likeness. All who suffer stretch out their arms like silhouettes of Calvary.

Thus the novelist Chaim Potok found that his broodings about suffering led him to create Asher Lev, "an observant Jew working on a crucifixion because there was no aesthetic mold in his own religious tradition into which he could pour a painting of ultimate anguish and torment."[1] The binding of Isaac was not enough. Asher Lev had to embrace the symbol that portrayed evil triumphant, gave the human sufferer no stay of execution, no victory other than commending his spirit into God's hands. That is all sufferers' most basic triumph.

Finally, a man may find his physical problems, emotional distress, and struggles to discover religious meaning compounded by the thoughtlessness of his doctors, the pettiness of his friends. Not seeing him whole, focusing mainly on his arteries and valves, his doctor may forget to explain things thoroughly, fail to be there when his anxieties are high. His friends, giving play to an ugly sense of superiority in being well, or an envy at the man's good fortune in other areas, may joke about his hypochondria, almost enjoy his emotional swings. This human obtuseness and rejoicing at others' misfortunes is at the center of our heart of darkness. It lurks uncharted and forbidding, like deepest Africa. Therefore the person suffering from it is forced to a very deep level of religious acceptance: he or she must forgive his or her enemies. Whether they do or do not know what they are doing, he or she will find his or her best peace by forgiving them.

At that point, suffering truly has become purifying. Like Jesus the high priest, the person has learned obedience, come to drink whatever chalice God gives. It is easy to tell God with our lips that we want his will to be done. Only suffering for God's will, ceding our own will through pain and fear, makes us genuine believers, people of heart and deed.

Forgiveness

Mercifully, God is the lead actor in the drama of forgiveness. Before we take the first step to unharden our hearts, God has come up to our door. Christians have treasured this ultimate revelation that God is love since Jesus gave them their beginning, but it remains an inexhaustible well. For a holistic spirtuality, it can be both a rock and a foundation. If God is slow to anger and quick to forgive as Exodus 34 insists, what need even the most fragmented of us fear? Having given us forgiveness incarnate, the full self-emptying of his Son, how can the Father fail to give us all other good gifts? A beautiful nature, a prosperous economy, a challenging polity, a supportive community—God's forgiveness makes them all quite possible. The same with a healthy diet, a playful contemplation, a warming sex, a maturing education, a meditation rooted in the Spirit's consolations. If God forgives us, keeps open his arms, says a fresh start is always possible, then the life of faith is a hundredfold now, an eternity of wholeness hereafter.

I do not mean this merely as rhetoric. I think it bears good analytical weight. For example, the person contemplating nature amidst God's forgiveness perceives creation differently than any alienated observer can. Nature is vast and I, a regenerate sinner, am very, very small. All praise then to the Creator of this beautiful vastness, all seconding of the angels' applause. Once, in the middle of Ignatius' *Spiritual Exercises,* I beheld the sea crashing against the Gloucester rocks, sending spray fifty feet high. Ever since, the sea has brought me the paradoxes of God's power, the awesome force of God's tenderness. The might that sent the spray flying, the breath-taking green and white, went so gently with my soreness that even my death now beckons kindly, a small final price to pay.

Social problems probably vex us more than natural, although ecology blends the two, but social problems also change, when our God is a forgiver. Consider the regenerative power of nature, how it can cleanse itself, how it wants to fight back. Consider the regenerative power of people, the slums that have returned to life. Very few of our economic, political, or community problems are terminal. Almost all can be cured, if we but muster the will to conversion. In a decade Jews and Palestinians could be allies, were forgiveness to seize them mutually. The United States and the Soviet Union could break the back of the arms race. Change a few images, get a few leaders, and what rapidly built up could rapidly break down. There is no necessary doomsday. God forgives us. We could forgive one another. We need not be prisoners of the past. God is an opener of futures. So hear ye, hear ye, hear ye: If God has so loved us, we ought so to love one another, give up the pleasures of hating.

Personal problems, of head or heart, of course also can change. Let God be a God of the living, a love that recreates and repairs, and today I can begin to eat sanely, love my spouse and my self healingly. I need not injure my body. My mind can play new tapes. The sex I hurry can go slowly. I hold the clock and the phone. As God slows time for me, stops the onrush of karma, so I can slow time for my beloved, put the clock and phone in the drawer. We need not rehash old failures. Old failures have had enough glory. We need not lash our psyches again. The God who forgives calls rehashing self-indulgence. So let's get on with it, try really to believe Jesus' good news. Let's study and pray as though the Spirit actually were never constrained. In a half hour, the Bible or *The Cloud* could completely transform us. Stranger things have befallen our children. At a single sitting our hearts might grow warm, even explode in a flash of recognition, as we see him in the breaking of the bread.

Ludwig Wittgeinstein, the pioneer philosopher of language, thought that the limits of our language were the limits of our world. Analogously, the limits of our images are the limits of our God. If we accept the biblical thesaurus of figures, God is never dead-ended. The only sin God cannot forgive is our closing to the Spirit of forgiveness. Only when we refuse to hope, give up trying, insist that God is as feeble as we, do the heavens close against us, the gates of regeneration slam. God will not force our hoping. We do have to fight for our lives. But our part is so very small, the scales tilt so completely in our favor, that only the smallest fraction of us must fail to win, only the tiniest portion end badly.

It could, of course, be very different. The majority might end in a howling abyss. There is nothing necessary in God's forgiveness. Always and everywhere we have nothing to boast. Yet, *de facto*, God has chosen to be our forgiver. Speculation aside, the reality is a human existence everywhere graced. And the warrant for this audacious assertion, the proof for what seems too good to be true? Nothing but Christ crucified and risen, the power and wisdom of God. If Christ is true, we are forgiven. If Jesus is Lord, God has won. Once and for all, history moves toward a blessed consummation, however mysterious its wherefores and hows. True, one should not say these things lightly, risk any cheapening of grace. But, equally truly, no Christian should fail to say these things boldly, regularly, self-deprecatingly, so that God may be all in all.

Divinization

The forgiveness of God takes most of us beyond what we easily accredit, but forgiveness is not God's final word. For traditional Christian theology grace is not only healing *(gratia sanans)*, it is also divinizing *(gratia elevans)*. The same love that binds up our psychic wounds, fills in our pockmarks and hollows, lifts us up into God's life, makes us sharers of the very divine nature (2 Pet 1:4).

Since love is a force for union, an energy seeking to make two into one, we may think of the love of God as a force for divine union, an energy seeking to sublate our humanity into God's divinity. How this can be so we can only sense most dimly. The heights of God's love are far too distant for our earthly eyes. But that this is so sings through all the New Testament and early Christian era: God has done a splendid new thing, poured out love beyond our wildest inklings. What eye has not seen, ear not heard, it not entered our hearts to conceive, that God has not only promised but accomplished, not only pledged but brought about once and for all.

The center of grace is not God's help, not even God's detoxification of our sin. The center of grace is God's own love-life, the substantial stuff of the Trinitarian processes. What circulates among Father, Son, and Spirit circulates in the minds, hearts, and spirits of God's people. If we are not our own in virtue of creation, in virtue of grace, we are triply not our own. Another holds the key to our meaning, the title to our hearts, the career that will absorb us for the future. The troubler of Israel, become the consoler of all who weep, has made our fate, our lives, our beings his personal own. The covenant, keystone of the Old Testament theology, has become what Jeremiah hoped it might be: new, interior, written on the fleshy tablets of the human heart. As a result, we live now not we but Father, Son, and Spirit live in us.

Can one take this quite traditional (although also quite neglected) theology of the Fathers and give it a contemporary, experiential diction? Certainly people bold enough to attempt holistic theologies will not hesitate to try. The life of God, concentric with our center, perfects our human natures. That is staple Catholic teaching, well integrated with the hopeful view of human nature, and analogous view of being, that long has characterized the Catholic tradition. Accepting this, one can suggest that the fathomlessness of the Father, his modality of unbegottenness, fosters an appreciation of nature's nearly infinite regression, the millions of light years into which the universe recedes. What those light years symbolize (we certainly can't imagine them with any concreteness) in the quantitative and physical orders, God the Father is qualitatively and spiritually. He is the storehouse, the reservoir, the inexhaustible font. So profound and creative is the paternal divine love that it can actualize any possibility, give breath and blood and warmth to anything that might stand in the light.

I have called this modality of the Trinitarian love paternal, because in Christian tradition the first, fontal "person" of the

Godhead has usually been called "Father." But other religious traditions (notably, Buddhism and Taoism) have spoken of this dimension of ultimate reality in feminine imagery: the cosmic womb, the Wisdom that begets all the Buddhas, the Tao as motherly love. If Christian theology stays open to feminist thought, or takes its dialogue with Eastern religions seriously, no doubt its future Trinitarian theology will try to incorporate such feminine imagery. Then the traditional notion that God is beyond sexual sterotypes may pay a much richer dividend.

Any way, as Father, Mother, or simply Parent, the depth of the Christian Godhead presses upon us to illumine the depths of our human appreciation, creativity, and oceanic awareness. If we can map the heavens, brood ground-level ontology, make endless poetic creations, we can do this still more perfectly, more beautifully, when we are uplifted by God's personal love. Our work, our contemplation, and the spread of our love beyond our sight all assume a further significance when God's embrace cushions them, God's yea-saying seconds their motions.

Similarly, we can hypothesize experiential overtones to our sharing in the relations of the Son and Holy Spirit. The light that flashes in our minds, the childhood that imprints our creatureliness, the iconic or sacramental quality that beautifies all our culture, the organic union of the branches in the vine—all these figures swell and dance beguilingly, when we set them in the context of divinization.

Further, our growing into the divine life, the early Christians' *theopoesis,* can be the base-motif of a knowing discernment of the life-cycle. Then the inmost significance of the identity, intimacy, generativity, and integrity that pace us through adulthood is the Spirit's holy nuptials. Traditionally the Spirit presides over the life-cycle journey as the "other helper" whom Jesus left. Groaning in our prayer, so that God himself finally makes our outcry to God, the Spirit circumincesses in our hearts, breathes forth love in our communities, as he does in the heavenly divine community. As Karl Rahner has phrased it, the economic Trinity (God active throughout creation) and the immanent Trinity (God complete unto himself) are completely one and the same. What we get now is what we shall see then in a coruscant, beatifying vision. What we are now, especially in our knowing and loving, is what God always is fully, splendidly, without let, hindrance, or flaw. And by God's grace, this splendor seeps into all our graces: whatever is noble, kindly, insightful, creative, or lovely about us God caresses so gently, so proudly, that one might call him a nursing Mother.

A Day in the Life of a Holistic Christian

Where sin abounded, grace has abounded the more: that is the holistic Christian's main slogan. The love of God at the center of Jesus' preaching and person is at least latent in all the dimensions of human living. We go into no dimension unpreceded by God, need consider none foreign or hostile. Still, the practical question remains: How can I boil this down, compact and point it, to start making holism a pattern of daily living? Consider the following sketch one tentative answer to that question.

A holistic day might shape itself like a Christian mandala. I try to put meditations at the beginning and the end, giving the central portions over to hard work. So, rising early, greeting the sun, I try to reset my hopes and goals. Today is another opportunity to grow in God's love, manifest God's love, learn how God's love spreads throughout creation. If I am worried or harried, think the day likely will be testing, I try to offer my worry to God, let the Spirit again file down my false fears or ambitions. What matters in this day, as in any day, is not my will but God's. My part is to do what I can, easily and graciously. Maybe today will mainly be suffering: frustration, disappointment, things not going well. Maybe someone will need my help: kindness, competence, eyes that see. Whatever, this day can be an adventure, if I will to see it as such. So come, Creator Spirit, visit this mind that belongs to you; give me the strength of your love.

On to breakfast, my first set of choices about diet and health. I like to think of nutrition rather than speed, fuels that burn steadily rather than quick fixes of sugar and caffeine. Then off to work, where I find most of my social issues. If I choose my work well, its inertia takes me toward economic justice, participatory politics, community relations that fire and support. To teach, heal, engineer, defend at the bar, or make beautiful things in a spirit of justice and helpfulness is to bend work toward the service of Christ's kingdom. To feed, clothe, repair, or counsel as though people were members of one another, radical equals, is to baptize work and make it whole. The ways that we buy and sell, collaborate and give service, weave crucial patterns in all our brains. Since most people don't retreat to consider the world globally or move down to ultimate forces like creation and grace, most people's "reality" depends on how their economic and social experiences go forward, whether we make them feel helped or screwed to the wall. Those of us (no doubt the majority) who must work in institutions seriously flawed, quite incompatible with Christ's high standards, must try especially hard to be honest, thoughtful, and courteous. This will not make a bad institution, part of the problem of poverty and suffering, good, but it will somewhat redeem both it and our work.

In the middle of the day I try to grab some hard exercise. (This time may be impossible for you, so consider a time before or after work.) I like to exercise in the middle of the day because it divides the pressures of my work, gets me out of my head and back to my body. So, at least three weekdays, I drag myself to the track and try to put in five steady miles. Usually I begin reluctantly and end gratefully (oxygenation becoming a minor sacrament). I blow off steam, take off weight, and try to reverence my Creator with my body. Usually a light lunch is quite enough and the second half of my work goes much better. My spirits rise, I burn off depression, and I'm glad to be one of God's animals.

Evenings I think are for family, culture, strolls in the park, talks neath the moon. Like the morning, the evening usually is quiet, conducive to centering down. Before retiring, I go over the day's doings, try to discern what its spirits have been. If a tactic has worked well, a difficult problem resolved itself, I like to note it for the future. If something went badly, made an irritating mess, I like to note that also, so as not to make the same mistake again. Then I try to bend this reflection, this examination of conscience,[2] toward simple abiding with my God. I ask forgiveness for my waywardness, offer thanks for all God's gifts, and try to linger, abide, love heart to heart. When this goes well I end peacefully, rhythmically, simply following the intake and out-flow of my breath.

Often the final bit of holism that makes the day ideal is a sharing of sexual love. Having this follow upon peaceful prayer seems to make it all the more nourishing. True, I also like morning times, vacation times, spontaneous flurries in the sunspace. But often the night's easy, tired, relaxed mutuality is the simplest and the sweetest. Gently, we console, connect, harmonize, give over. Thankfully we finish the day whole, round, much as God created us: male and female, just the complement the other needs.

Satisfaction leads to peace, peace leads to sleep. In a dark night, our houses having come to rest, we slip away from consciousness, anticipate death, go back to the abyss of pre-creation. A sleep of unknowing reknits our raveled care. Another day has turned, another sun gone down, taking us closer to our destiny. If, day by day, more becomes well, more becomes whole, our final destiny will be splendid.

Notes

Chapter One
   1. Robert Coles, *Privileged Ones* (Boston: Little, Brown, 1977), pp. 548–549.
   2. See John Updike, *Rabbit Is Rich* (New York: Fawcett Crest, 1981).
   3. See Alexsandr I. Solzhenitsyn, *East & West* (New York: Harper & Row, 1980), pp. 35–36.

Chapter Two
   1. Annie Dillard, *Pilgrim at Tinker Creek* (New York: Harper's Magazine Press, 1974).
   2. For a beginning see John Carmody, *Ecology and Religion: Toward a New Christian Theology of Nature* (Ramsey, N.J.: Paulist Press, 1983).
   3. See *Transcendence and the Sacred*, ed. Alan M. Olson (Notre Dame, Ind.: University of Notre Dame Press, 1981).
   4. Colin M. Turnbull, *The Forest People* (New York: Simon & Schuster, 1962), p. 92.
   5. *Ibid.*, pp. 92–93.
   6. See Colin M. Turnbull, *The Mountain People* (New York: Simon & Schuster, 1972).
   7. *Ibid.*, p. 188.
   8. C. G. Jung, *Memories, Dreams, Reflections* (New York: Vintage, 1963), p. 250.

Chapter Three

1. See Eric Fromm, *Marx's Concept of Man* (New York: Frederick Ungar, 1961); José Miranda, *Marx Against the Marxists* (Maryknoll, N.Y.: Orbis, 1980); Arthur McGovern, *Marxism: An American Christian Perspective* (Maryknoll, N.Y.: Orbis, 1980).

2. E. F. Schumacher, *Small Is Beautiful* (New York: Harper & Row, 1973).

3. Robert Heilbroner, *Marxism: For and Against* (New York: W. W. Norton, 1980), especially pp. 95–105.

4. See Tu Wei-Ming, "The Confucian Perception of Adulthood," In *Adulthood*, ed. Erik Erikson (New York: W.W. Norton, 1978), pp. 113–127.

5. See, for example, G. Tyler Miller, *Living in the Environment*, Third Edition (Belmont, Cal: Wadsworth, 1982).

Chapter Four

1. Diego de Gaspar, "Economics and World Hunger," in *Faith and Science in an Unjust World*, Vol. 1, ed. Roger Shinn (Philadelphia: Fortress, 1980), p. 227.

2. Americans For Democratic Action, *500 Days: ADA Assesses the Reagan Administration* (Washington, D.C.: Americans for Democratic Action, 1982), p. 20.

3. David Hollenbach, *Claims in Conflict* (Ramsey, N.J.: Paulist Press, 1979), p. 204.

4. *Puebla and Beyond*, ed. John Eagleson and Philip Scharper (Maryknoll, N.Y.: Orbis, 1979), p. 135.

5. See Ernesto Cardenal, *The Gospel in Solentiname* (Maryknoll, N.Y.: Orbis, 1976ff.).

Chapter Five

1. See Joan Meyer Anzia and Mary G. Durkin, *Marital Intimacy* (Kansas City, Mo.: Andrews and McMeel, 1980).

2. See the *Proceedings* of the Catholic Theological Society of America, Volume 36 (1981). The 1981 CTSA Convention focused on the local church.

3. See *The Challenge of Basic Christian Communities*, ed. Sergio Torres and John Eagleson (Maryknoll, N.Y.: Orbis, 1981).

4. Sobering is Igor Shafarevich's *The Socialist Phenomenon* (New York: Harper & Row, 1980).

5. Useful at this point might be James J. Bacik, *Apologetics and the Eclipse of Mystery* (Notre Dame, Ind.: University of Notre Dame Press, 1980), and Diogenes Allen, *The Traces of God* (Cambridge, Ma.: Cowley, 1981). On Wiesel see Robert McAfee Brown, *Elie Wiesel, Messenger to All Humanity* (Notre Dame, Ind.: University of Notre Dame Press, 1983).

Chapter Six

1. On the ecological aspects of meatless cooking, see Frances Moore Lappé, *Diet for a Small Planet*, Revised Edition (New York: Ballantine, 1975).

2. Jane Brody, *Jane Brody's Nutrition Book* (New York: W.W. Norton, 1981), p. 13.

3. *Ibid.*, p. 14.

4. See Donald Ardell, *14 Days to a Wellness Lifestyle* (Mill Valley, Cal.: Whatever Publishing, 1982).

5. James S. Gordon, "The Paradigm of Holistic Medicine," in *Health for the Whole Person*, ed. A. Hastings, J. Fadiman, and J. Gordon (New York: Bantam, 1981), p. 9.

6. See *ibid.*, pp. 17–26; also Patricia Anne Randolph Flynn, *Holistic Health* (Bowie, Md.: Robert J. Brady Co., 1980).

7. See *op. cit.*, p. 241.

Chapter Eight

1. For literary stimulus, see John Updike, *Rabbit Is Rich* (New York: Fawcett Crest, 1981).

2. Dorothy Dinnerstein, *The Mermaid and the Minotaur* (New York: Harper & Row, 1976).

3. Doris Lessing, *The Marriages Between Zones Three, Four, and Five* (New York: Alfred A. Knopf, 1980).

Chapter Nine

1. Albert Einstein, *The World As I See It* (New York: Citadel, n.d.), p. 28.

2. Lewis Thomas, *The Medusa and the Snail* (New York: Viking, 1979), p. 8.

3. See David Tracy, *The Analogical Imagination* (New York: Crossroad, 1981).

4. Bernard Lonergan, *Method in Theology* (New York: Herder & Herder, 1972).

5. For a general text in the spirit of communications theology, see Denise Lardner Carmody and John Tully Carmody, *Christianity: An Introduction* (Belmont, Cal: Wadsworth, 1983).

Chapter Ten

1. See, for example, William Johnston, *The Mirror Mind* (New York: Harper & Row, 1981); Anthony de Mello, *Sadhana: A Way to God* (St. Louis: Institute of Jesuit Sources, 1978). For a brief introduction to world religions that compares the traditions (especially Christianity and Buddhism) on many of the points treated in this book, see Denise Lardner Carmody and John Tully Carmody, *Religion: The Great Questions* (New York: Seabury, 1983).

2. *The Dhammapada*, trans. Juan Mascaro (Baltimore: Penguin, 1973), vv. 1–5, p. 35.

3. *Tao Te Ching*, trans. D. C. Lau (Baltimore: Penguin, 1963), chapter xliv, p. 105.

4. Philip Kapleau, *Zen: Dawn in the West* (Garden City, N.Y.: Doubleday/Anchor Press, 1980), pp. 15–16.

5. On spiritual direction, see William A. Barry and William J. Connolly, *The Practice of Spiritual Direction* (New York: Seabury, 1982). For an imaginative amalgam of the Eastern and Western traditions, see Roger Corless, *The Art of Christian Alchemy: Transfiguring the Ordinary through Holistic Meditation* (Ramsey, N.J.: Paulist Press, 1981).

6. See, for example, Harvey D. Egan, S.J., *The Spiritual Exercises and the Ignatian Mystical Horizon* (St. Louis: The Institute of Jesuit Sources, 1976).

7. See, for example, Thomas Keating, O.C.S.O. *et al.*, *Finding Grace at the Center* (Still River, Ma.: St. Bede Publications, 1978).

8. See Vladimir Lossky, *The Mystical Theology of the Eastern Church* (Crestwood, N.Y.: St. Vladimir's Seminary Press, 1976).

9. Sergius Bolshakoff and M. Basil Pennington, O.C.S.O., *In Search of True Wisdom: Visits to Eastern Spiritual Fathers* (Garden City, N.Y.: Doubleday, 1979), p. 171.

10. Harvey D. Egan, S.J., *What Are They Saying About Mysticism?* (Ramsey, N.J.: Paulist Press, 1982), p. 98.

Chapter Eleven
1. Chaim Potok, *My Name Is Asher Lev* (New York: Alfred A. Knopf, 1972), p. 330.
2. Elsewhere I have sketched a full spiritual regime in terms of the examination of conscience. See John Carmody, *Reexamining Conscience* (New York: Seabury, 1982).

Annotated Bibliography

American Friends Service Committee, *A Compassionate Peace* (New York: Hill and Wang, 1982). An analysis of the Middle Eastern crisis that could serve as a paradigm for the sort of balanced, sensitive, yet radical political science that Christian faith ought to inspire.

Ardell, Donald, *14 Days to a Wellness Lifestyle* (Mill Valley, Cal: Whatever Publishing, 1982). A well-known writer on health offers self-help in two weeks that could make one eat better, exercise better, and think more wholesome thoughts.

Barry, William A., and Connolly, William J., *The Practice of Spiritual Direction* (New York: Seabury, 1982). A positive view, well-informed by clinical psychology and Ignatian spirituality, from two of the founders of the Center for Religious Development in Cambridge, Massachusetts.

Bolshakoff, Sergius and Pennington, M. Basil, *In Search of True Wisdom: Visits to Eastern Spiritual Fathers* (Garden City, N.Y.: Doubleday, 1979). Insightful interviews with Russian and Greek Orthodox spiritual masters that bring out the Eastern stress on divinization and the Jesus Prayer.

Brody, Jane, *Jane Brody's Nutrition Book* (New York: W.W. Norton, 1981). The personal health columnist of the New York Times puts together a large, basic volume dealing with everything from abortion to zinc.

Brown, Raymond E., *The Community of the Beloved Disciple* (New York: Paulist Press, 1979). A study of the community behind the Johannine literature that offers an encouraging view of the strife-torn process by which the New Testament's most profound meditations on love emerged.

Cardenal, Ernesto, *The Gospel in Solentiname* (Maryknoll, N.Y.: Orbis, 1976ff.). A multi-volumed collection of the dialogue-sermons of the little Nicaraguan grass-roots community that so threatened Somoza that he had his soldiers burn it down.

Carmody, Denise Lardner, *Feminism and Christianity: A Two-Way Reflection* (Nashville: Abingdon, 1982). A centrist analysis of the implications that feminism and Christianity bear one another.

Carmody, John, *Ecology and Religion: Toward a New Christian Theology of Nature* (Ramsey, N.J.: Paulist Press, 1983). A survey of recent discussions of the full range of ecological problems and a Lonerganian sketch of how the functional specialties of theology might forge a new religious conception of nature.

Carmody, John, *Reexamining Conscience* (New York: Seabury, 1982). A sketch of a lay spiritual regime pivoted on the interaction between daily worldly experience and nightly reflection before God.

Carmody, John, *The Heart of the Christian Matter* (Nashville: Abingdon, 1983). An ecumenical introduction to Christianity that draws on the Protestant, Roman Catholic, and Orthodox traditions and focuses on Jesus, love of God, and love of neighbor.

Catholic Theological Society of America, *Human Sexuality* (Garden City, N.Y.: Doubleday/Anchor, 1979). A controversial report on new trends in American Catholic thought about sexuality.

Cooper, Kenneth, *The New Aerobics* (New York: Bantam, 1970). The pioneer theoretician of jogging offers a persuasive rationale for attaining cardiovascular fitness.

Doherty, Dennis, ed., *Dimensions of Human Sexuality* (Garden City, N.Y.: Doubleday, 1979). Essays responding to *Human Sexuality* that round out the Christian theology of sex.

Egan, Harvey D., *What Are They Saying About Mysticism?* (Ramsey, N.J.: Paulist Press, 1982). A fine survey of recent discussions of mysticism that provides a good context for a holistic treatment of prayer and holiness.

Freire, Paulo, *Pedagogy of the Oppressed* (New York: Seabury, 1970). The pioneer work showing the pedagogical implications of Latin American liberation theology.

Grollenberg, Lucas, *Jesus* (Philadelphia: Westminster, 1978). A simple, winning portrait of Jesus that spotlights his humanity and utter trust in his Father.

Groome, Thomas H., *Christian Religious Education* (San Francisco: Harper & Row, 1980). A view of Christian religious education that stresses the theology of story, developmental psychology, and the dynamics of community.

Hastings, Arthur C., *et al.*, eds., *Health for the Whole Person* (New York: Bantam, 1981). A reader in holistic medicine that touches base with all the component parts and offers useful bibliographies.

Haughey, John C., ed., *The Faith That Does Justice* (New York: Paulist Press/Woodstock, 1977). Essays on the theology of politics and social justice that reflect the Catholic tradition of the social encyclicals.

Heilbroner, Robert L., *Marxism: For and Against* (New York: W.W. Norton, 1980). A liberal economist offers a balanced assessment of Marxist economics, in full awareness of the dim prospects for human survival.

Hollenbach, David, *Claims in Conflict* (New York: Paulist Press, 1979). A fine survey of recent Roman Catholic social thought with solid suggestions for its future development.

Janovy, John, Jr., *Keith County Journal* (New York: St Martin's, 1978). A professor at the University of Nebraska tramps the fields and makes their teeming life our own ecological niche.

Johnston, William, *The Inner Eye of Love* (San Francisco: Harper & Row, 1978). A warm Loncrganian treatment of religious experience and prayer by a student of both Zen and the *Cloud of Unknowing*.

Lekachman, Robert, *Greed Is Not Enough* (New York: Pantheon, 1982). A devastating critique of Reaganomics.

Miller, G. Tyler, *Living in the Environment*, Third Edition (Belmont, Cal.: Wadsworth, 1982). A wonderful college text, beautifully illustrated, that presents the basic data about the study of ecology and the current state of our various ecosystems.

Polanyi, Michael, *Personal Knowledge* (New York: Harper & Row, 1964). The personalist epistemology, stressing the tacit dimension of knowing, that I would make central in a philosophy of education.

Potok, Chaim, *My Name Is Asher Lev* (New York: Alfred A. Knopf, 1972). A Jewish novelist depicts the artistic life and its religious entailments.

Rahner, Karl, *Foundations of Christian Faith* (New York: Seabury Crossroad, 1978). A difficult but rewarding view of the whole span of Christian theology by the master whose views of grace have most informed the present work.

Schumacher, E. F., *Good Work* (New York: Harper & Row, 1979). The leading theoretician of the combine of work, ecology, economics, and Christian spirituality offers holistic insights about life, faith, and work.

Sheehan, George, *Running and Being* (New York: Simon and Schuster, 1978). Medical and philosophical reflections on running by one of the gurus of *Runner's World*.

Torres, Sergio, and Eagleson, John, eds., *The Challenge of Basic Christian Communities* (Maryknoll, N.Y.: Orbis, 1981). Papers from the 1980 International Ecumenical Congress of Theology in São Paulo, Brazil that focused on the political, liturgical, and theological experiences of small Christian groups living in circumstances of oppression.

Whitehead, Evelyn Eaton, and Whitehead, James D., *Christian Life Patterns* (Garden City, N.Y.: Doubleday, 1979). A Christian adaptation of the life-cycle studies of Erikson and his successors that describes how faith might develop through adulthood.